Unity 3D for Beginners: Game Development from Scratch

Create Stunning Games with C# and the Unity Engine

Greyson Chesterfield

COPYRIGHT

DISCLAIMER

The information provided in this book is for general informational purposes only. All content in this book reflects the author's views and is based on their research, knowledge, and experiences. The author and publisher make no representations or warranties of any kind concerning the completeness, accuracy, reliability, suitability, or availability of the information contained herein.

This book is not intended to be a substitute for professional advice, diagnosis, or treatment. Readers should seek professional advice for any specific concerns or conditions. The author and publisher disclaim any liability or responsibility for any direct, indirect, incidental, or consequential loss or damage arising from the use of the information contained in this book.

Contents

Introduction to Unity and Game Development

Overview of Game Development

Game development is one of the most exciting and rapidly growing fields in the tech industry. Whether you're playing a mobile app, exploring a 3D adventure on your console, or battling enemies in a multiplayer game, there's a team of talented individuals behind the scenes who have worked tirelessly to bring those experiences to life. For the uninitiated, the world of game development can seem vast and complex, but it's also a place where creativity meets technology, and anyone with the right tools and dedication can make their vision a reality.

At the core of game development lies a combination of several disciplines: coding, graphic design, audio engineering, and game mechanics design. Each of these plays a vital role in the creation of a game, but it all starts with one thing — **the game engine**. A game engine is a software framework designed to simplify the development of video games. It provides developers with the tools to create, design, and manage all the elements needed to build a game. This includes graphics rendering, physics simulations, sound integration, and even scripting for the game logic.

Game engines allow developers to focus on creating fun and engaging gameplay rather than reinventing the wheel for every new project. One of the most popular and accessible game engines today is **Unity**.

Why Unity?

Unity is a powerful game development engine that has become a staple for both beginners and seasoned professionals alike. Founded in 2005, Unity Technologies designed the engine to be versatile, user-friendly, and accessible to developers of all skill levels. Today, Unity powers some of the world's most beloved games, including *Angry Birds 2*, *Pokemon Go*, *Monument Valley*, and many others. Its versatility has earned it a reputation as a go-to platform for creating everything from small indie games to large-scale AAA titles.

So why is Unity such a dominant force in game development?

1. **Cross-Platform Support**: One of Unity's most appealing features is its ability to export games to a wide variety of platforms. Whether you're creating a mobile game, a desktop game, or even a virtual reality (VR) or augmented reality (AR) experience, Unity allows you to easily export your project to multiple platforms such as iOS, Android, Windows, macOS, PlayStation, Xbox, WebGL, and more. This cross-platform capability saves developers valuable time and resources as they don't have to reinvent their games for each platform individually.

2. **User-Friendly Interface**: Unity has always been known for its beginner-friendly interface. While other engines can be intimidating for newcomers,

Unity's layout is intuitive, with drag-and-drop functionality, visual tools, and easy-to-navigate menus. Its approachability allows developers to focus on creativity rather than getting bogged down by technical hurdles.

3. **Comprehensive Documentation and Community Support**: Unity has a vast library of tutorials, documentation, and support forums, making it one of the most beginner-friendly engines on the market. The Unity community is large and active, so if you run into any issues, chances are, someone has already solved them and posted about it online.

4. **C# Scripting**: Unity uses C#, one of the most widely used programming languages in the world. C# is known for being clean, powerful, and relatively easy to learn. For beginners, the C# scripting environment in Unity allows you to learn programming fundamentals while also seeing immediate results within the game engine. It's a great way to get your feet wet in the world of programming without feeling overwhelmed.

5. **Asset Store**: Unity's Asset Store is a goldmine for developers, offering thousands of pre-made assets, tools, and templates that can help speed up the development process. Whether you need character models, environments, sound effects, or even entire game templates, the Asset Store can help you cut down on development time, allowing you to focus on what really matters — your game's design and mechanics.

6. **Real-Time Rendering**: Unity's real-time rendering capabilities allow developers to see how their game looks and behaves while they're building it. This is especially valuable for designing levels, animations, and environments, as developers can instantly test and tweak their creations.

The Appeal of Game Development with Unity

Game development offers a unique opportunity to blend creativity and technology. As a developer, you're not just writing lines of code or creating assets — you're designing immersive experiences that captivate and engage players. Unity provides a rich environment for both novice and experienced developers to craft these experiences.

The best part? You don't need to have a big budget or a large team to get started with Unity. The Unity engine itself is free to use for small projects, making it an ideal choice for hobbyists, independent developers, and newcomers who want to learn the ropes without investing a lot of money upfront.

The ability to prototype quickly, iterate, and see the fruits of your labor almost immediately is one of the most exciting aspects of Unity. For beginners, the platform allows you to quickly get into game creation, and for professionals, it's a powerful tool that enables the development of high-quality, polished games.

But getting started can sometimes feel daunting. Even with an engine as user-friendly as Unity, it's easy to feel overwhelmed by the number of features and options available. This is where our book comes in. We will guide you through each step of your game development journey, ensuring that you build the foundation you need to create your very own game, from scratch, using Unity and C#.

How This Book is Structured

This book is designed to take you from a beginner, someone who has never opened Unity or written a line of code, all the way to creating your very first complete game. The structure of the book is aimed at gradual learning, ensuring that you build both your knowledge and confidence as you progress through each chapter. With clear explanations, practical exercises, and real-world examples, you'll find yourself steadily developing your skills and expanding your understanding of both Unity and game development.

Here's how we'll guide you through the process:

Chapter 1: Getting Started with Unity

We'll begin by introducing you to Unity itself. You'll learn how to install the Unity Hub, set up your first project, and familiarize yourself with the Unity interface. We'll break down the core components of the Unity Editor, such as the Scene view, Game view, Hierarchy, Project window, and Inspector, helping you get comfortable navigating the environment. By the end of this chapter, you'll have Unity set up and ready to start creating your first game.

Chapter 2: The Basics of C# for Unity

While Unity provides the framework for your game, C# is the language you'll use to bring your game to life. In this chapter, we'll introduce you to the fundamentals of C# programming. You'll learn how to write simple scripts that control in-game objects, such as moving a player character or interacting with items. Don't worry — you won't need to know how to program before starting. We'll explain every concept in simple, clear terms, and you'll have plenty of opportunities to practice with hands-on examples.

Chapter 3: Creating Your First Game Scene

Now that you're familiar with Unity and C#, we'll dive into the actual creation of your first game scene. You'll learn how to place objects like cubes, spheres, and cameras in the 3D world. Then, you'll make those objects interactive, such as by allowing a player character to move around using keyboard inputs. At this point, you'll start to see how all the pieces come together, and you'll feel a real sense of accomplishment as your first game world begins to take shape.

Chapter 4: Working with Game Objects and Components

Unity is built around the concept of **GameObjects**, which are the basic building blocks of any Unity scene. Every character, item, and environmental object in your game is a GameObject. This chapter will introduce you to the most important components of GameObjects, including Rigidbody (for physics interactions), Colliders (for detecting collisions), and Scripts (for adding behavior). You'll learn how to add and manipulate these components to control the behavior of your objects in the game world.

Chapter 5: Building Player Movement

At this point, you'll have a basic game world, but now it's time to make things interactive. In this chapter, we'll teach you how to control player movement using the keyboard and mouse. You'll learn how to write code that allows your player to move in three-dimensional space, jump, and interact with objects. This is the core of any game, as player movement is the fundamental interaction that drives gameplay.

Chapter 6: Creating Simple Game Logic

With player movement in place, we'll explore how to add logic to your game. We'll introduce you to concepts like **game states**, **win conditions**, and **game over scenarios**. You'll learn how to create a simple scoring system, keep track of the player's health, and create the rules for advancing to the next level.

Chapter 7: Adding Audio and Visual Effects

Every great game is more than just functionality; it's about creating an immersive experience. This chapter will focus on enhancing your game with sound effects and visual effects. You'll learn how to add background music, sound effects for actions (like jumping, shooting, or collecting items), and how to make your game visually engaging through animations and particle effects.

Chapter 8: Designing Your First Level

Level design is one of the most exciting aspects of game development. In this chapter, you'll learn how to design your first playable level. We'll walk you through the process of creating obstacles, setting up a player path, and integrating challenges that make your game fun to play.

Chapter 9: Debugging and Polishing

Once your game starts to take shape, it's time to ensure that everything works as expected. In this chapter, we'll cover how to use Unity's debugging tools to identify and fix any issues in your code. You'll also learn how to optimize your game for better performance and polish it to make it as smooth and engaging as possible.

Chapter 10: Exporting and Publishing Your Game

The final step is taking your game from concept to reality. We'll walk you through the process of exporting your game for different platforms, from PC and macOS to mobile devices and the web. You'll also learn how to prepare your game for publishing and distribution.

By the end of this book, you will have the skills and confidence to create your own games using Unity and C#. You'll have learned the basics of game development, from setting up your first project to designing and publishing a complete game. Whether you want to develop your skills further or jump straight into creating larger, more complex games, this book will provide you with the foundation you need to succeed.

Chapter 1: Getting Started with Unity

What is Unity?

Unity is a powerful and widely-used game development engine that has been the driving force behind some of the most successful and innovative games in the industry. Since its initial release in 2005, Unity has grown from a niche tool for indie developers into one of the most robust and versatile platforms for creating both 2D and 3D games across a variety of platforms, including mobile, console, PC, and virtual reality (VR) environments.

Unity's History:

Unity Technologies, the company behind the engine, was founded by three former students from the Copenhagen IT University in Denmark. Their original goal was to make a game engine that was simple, affordable, and accessible to a broader audience, especially small studios and independent developers. The vision was clear: make game development more accessible by providing a platform that allowed developers to create cross-platform games efficiently, using a user-friendly interface.

At its inception, Unity was designed to target the Mac OS, and over time, it expanded to support multiple platforms, including Windows, Linux, and eventually iOS and

Android. Today, Unity supports over 25 platforms, ranging from consoles like PlayStation and Xbox to mobile devices, desktop computers, and even WebGL. It continues to evolve, supporting new technologies like augmented reality (AR) and virtual reality (VR), which have significantly expanded the possibilities for game development.

Unity was revolutionary for several reasons:

1. **Accessibility:** Unity's freemium model made it easy for hobbyists and independent developers to get started without significant financial investment. It's free to use for personal and small commercial projects.

2. **Cross-Platform Compatibility:** Unity's ability to export games to numerous platforms with minimal adjustments made it an attractive option for developers who wanted to reach a global audience across different devices.

3. **C# Scripting:** Unity uses C# (pronounced "C-sharp") for scripting, which is a powerful, high-level programming language that is easy to learn and widely used in the software development industry.

4. **Asset Store:** Unity's Asset Store provides a marketplace for developers to purchase and sell assets, ranging from 3D models and textures to fully functional game templates, reducing the amount of work needed for prototyping and developing assets from scratch.

5. **Real-Time Development:** Unity provides a real-time development environment, allowing

developers to see the results of their work immediately and make changes on the fly.

Over the years, Unity's focus has been on making the development process more efficient, accessible, and scalable for both indie developers and large studios. Unity is now used by everyone from small independent game developers to large AAA game studios, and its flexibility and power continue to make it a top choice for game developers around the world.

Installing Unity and Setting Up Your First Project

Before diving into creating your first game, the first step is to get Unity up and running on your computer. In this section, we'll walk you through the process of downloading and installing Unity using the **Unity Hub**.

1. Installing Unity Hub

Unity Hub is a central application that helps manage your Unity projects, installations, and licenses. It provides an easy way to download different versions of Unity, create new projects, and keep your tools organized.

Step-by-Step Installation:

1. **Download Unity Hub:**
   - Go to Unity's official website at unity.com and click on the "Get Started" button. You'll be asked whether you want to download Unity Hub. Choose the appropriate version

based on your operating system (Windows or macOS).

- o Download and run the installer. Follow the instructions on-screen to complete the installation.

2. **Create a Unity Account:**

- o Once Unity Hub is installed, you'll need to sign in using a Unity account. If you don't already have one, you can create a free account through Unity's website.

3. **Install a Unity Version:**

- o Unity Hub lets you manage multiple versions of Unity. For beginners, it's recommended to download the **latest stable version** of Unity.

- o In Unity Hub, click the "Installs" tab on the left side, and then click the "Add" button to choose a Unity version. You'll be prompted to select additional modules (e.g., support for iOS, Android, etc.). You can leave these at their default settings or select them based on your needs.

4. **Setting Up Your First Project:**

- o Once Unity is installed, return to the "Projects" tab in Unity Hub and click "New."

- o Choose a template for your first project. For beginners, we recommend starting with the

3D Template, as it will give you the flexibility to create both 2D and 3D games.

o Name your project and choose a location on your computer where you'd like to store it.

o Finally, click "Create." Unity will launch, and your new project will open in the Unity Editor, ready for development.

Understanding the Unity Interface

Unity's interface is where you'll spend most of your time as you build your game. It may seem overwhelming at first, but it's actually designed to be intuitive and flexible, allowing you to customize your workspace to suit your workflow. Let's take a closer look at the key components of the **Unity Editor**.

1. The Scene View

The **Scene View** is where you build and manipulate the elements that make up your game world. Think of it as the "workspace" where you lay out all of your objects, from characters to environments. The Scene View provides an interactive 3D environment where you can move, rotate, and scale objects, and it gives you an overview of how everything fits together. You can also navigate this view using your mouse to zoom in and out, or pan around to look at your scene from different angles.

- **Scene Navigation:** Use the right mouse button to rotate the view, the middle mouse button to pan, and the mouse wheel to zoom in and out.

- **Gizmos:** These are helpful visual tools that allow you to manipulate and control various game objects in the Scene View.

2. The Game View

While the Scene View shows the raw layout of your game world, the **Game View** is where you see what the player will experience in the game. This is a real-time preview of the game as it would appear when played, with all of the animations, physics, and gameplay elements active.

- **Play Mode:** The Game View works hand-in-hand with **Play Mode**. When you click the "Play" button (located at the top of the interface), your game runs in the Game View, and you can test the functionality and gameplay in real time.

- **Camera:** The Camera in Unity is the player's view of the game world. You can adjust the camera's position and orientation to change the perspective.

3. The Hierarchy Panel

The **Hierarchy** panel shows all the GameObjects in your current scene. GameObjects are the fundamental building blocks of Unity, representing everything in the game world, such as characters, environments, props, cameras, and lights. The Hierarchy panel organizes these objects in a tree structure, with parent-child relationships that help you understand how your objects are nested.

- **GameObjects:** Every item in your game world, from the ground to the player character, is a GameObject in Unity. Each GameObject has components that define its behavior and properties.

- **Scene Organization:** You can organize objects into different groups in the Hierarchy for better management, making it easier to find specific GameObjects and organize your scene.

4. The Inspector Panel

The **Inspector** is one of the most important panels in the Unity Editor. It provides a detailed view of the properties and components of the currently selected GameObject. When you select an object in the Hierarchy, the Inspector shows its various components (e.g., transforms, materials, physics properties, scripts) and allows you to modify them.

- **Component-based Design:** Unity's system is based on components that can be added to GameObjects. For example, a player character might have a Transform component (for its position, rotation, and scale), a Rigidbody component (for physics interactions), and a Collider component (for detecting collisions).

- **Editing Properties:** The Inspector allows you to modify these components directly. For instance, you can change the position of an object by adjusting the values in the Transform component.

5. The Project Panel

The **Project Panel** is where you manage all of the assets in your game project. It shows you a folder structure containing all of the files in your Unity project, such as 3D models, textures, scripts, and scenes.

- **Asset Management:** You can import new assets, organize them into folders, and create new files (like scripts and prefabs) right from the Project panel.

- **Drag-and-Drop Functionality:** You can drag assets from the Project Panel directly into the Scene View or the Inspector to attach them to GameObjects.

6. The Console Panel

The **Console** is where Unity logs messages related to your game's performance, errors, and warnings. As you develop your game and write scripts, any issues or messages that occur during gameplay will appear in the Console, helping you diagnose problems.

Real-World Example: The Unity Interface as a Digital Art Studio

To help you visualize how Unity works, think of it like a digital art studio where you, as the creator, are crafting a game world. The **Scene View** is your canvas, where you arrange and paint the elements of your game. These elements (GameObjects) are your brushes, tools, and materials that allow you to build a dynamic, interactive world. The **Inspector** is your palette, where you control the properties and details of each element you add to your scene.

The **Game View** is like stepping back and looking at your painting from a distance, seeing how all the colors, shapes, and objects come together to form a cohesive final piece. The **Hierarchy** is your list of supplies, ensuring that every brush and tool is accounted for and correctly placed. And the **Project Panel** is your storage area, where you organize your paints, textures, and models, so you can find them when you need them.

Just as a painter uses a variety of tools to create their work, in Unity, you use the Scene View, Game View, Hierarchy, Inspector, and Project Panel to create your game, tweak the details, and see the big picture come to life.

Chapter 2: The Basics of C# for Unity

Introduction to C#

Before we dive into coding in Unity, we need to familiarize ourselves with C#, the primary programming language used for scripting. C# (pronounced "C-sharp") is a modern, object-oriented programming language developed by Microsoft. It is widely used in the software development world, including for building games with Unity.

Why C# for Unity?

Unity chose C# because it is a robust and beginner-friendly language that offers both ease of use and powerful functionality. If you've had any prior experience with other programming languages, such as Python or Java, you'll find that C# shares many similar concepts, making it easier to learn.

While Unity provides a visual environment to design your game world, the scripting part—writing the code that controls the game logic—is done using C#. This is what makes your game interactive, responsive to player input, and able to behave in interesting and dynamic ways.

Core Concepts of C# for Unity

Let's break down the foundational concepts you'll need to understand to begin writing C# scripts for Unity.

1. Variables

A **variable** in programming is like a container that stores data. Each variable has a type (e.g., integer, float, string), which defines what kind of data it can store. Variables allow you to store values that your game will use, like the player's score, health, or position.

Here are some common types of variables in C#:

- **int:** Stores whole numbers (e.g., 5, -2, 100)

- **float:** Stores decimal numbers (e.g., 3.14, -0.5, 100.75)

- **string:** Stores text (e.g., "Hello", "Player 1")

- **bool:** Stores Boolean values (true or false)

Example of variable declaration:

csharp

```
int playerScore = 0;  // Integer variable to store the player's score

float playerSpeed = 5.5f;  // Float variable to store the player's speed

string playerName = "Player";  // String variable to store the player's name
```

bool isGameOver = false; // Boolean variable to store whether the game is over

2. Functions

A **function** (also called a method) is a block of code that performs a specific task. Functions allow you to group related commands together and call them whenever needed. In Unity, functions are frequently used to define what happens when a player presses a key, when an object collides with another, or when a game object is created.

Here is an example of a simple function:

csharp

```
void Start() {

    Debug.Log("Hello, Unity!"); // This will print "Hello, Unity!" to the Console when the game starts

}
```

- **void** means that this function doesn't return a value.
- **Start()** is a special Unity function that runs automatically when the game starts.
- **Debug.Log()** is used to print messages to the console.

3. Classes and Objects

A **class** is a blueprint for creating objects. Objects are instances of classes, and they contain the properties and behaviors defined in the class. A class can represent a game object, like a player character or an enemy, and it can contain variables (e.g., health, speed) and functions (e.g., move, jump).

In Unity, every script you write is associated with a class. When you attach a script to a game object, that object is referred to as an instance of the class.

Example:

csharp

```csharp
public class Player : MonoBehaviour {

    public int health = 100;  // Property to store the player's health


    void Update() {
        if (health <= 0) {
            Debug.Log("Game Over!");
        }
    }
}
```

In this example:

- **Player** is the class.

- **health** is a variable that represents the player's health.

- **Update()** is another special function that is called once per frame.

4. Comments

Comments in C# are notes or explanations in the code that are ignored by the compiler but are there to help you or others understand what the code is doing. They are an essential part of writing clean, understandable code.

Example of a comment:

csharp

```
// This is a single-line comment
/* This is a

  multi-line comment */
```

Writing Your First C# Script

Now that we have a basic understanding of variables, functions, and classes, it's time to write a simple script in Unity. In this section, we'll write a script that controls the movement of a player using the transform.Translate() function. This will give us an interactive game object that responds to player input.

Step-by-Step Guide: Creating the Script

1. **Create a New Script in Unity:**

   o Open Unity and navigate to the **Project Panel**.

   o Right-click in the **Assets** folder and choose **Create → C# Script**.

- o Name the script PlayerMovement.

2. **Edit the Script:**

   - o Double-click the PlayerMovement.cs script to open it in your preferred code editor (Visual Studio or Visual Studio Code).

   - o Delete the default code and add the following code to move the player with the arrow keys or the WASD keys:

csharp

```csharp
using UnityEngine;

public class PlayerMovement : MonoBehaviour {
    public float moveSpeed = 5.0f;  // Variable to control player movement speed

    // Update is called once per frame
    void Update() {
        float horizontal = Input.GetAxis("Horizontal");  // Get input from arrow keys or A/D

        float vertical = Input.GetAxis("Vertical");  // Get input from W/S or arrow keys

        Vector3 moveDirection = new Vector3(horizontal, 0, vertical);  // Define the movement direction
```

```
    transform.Translate(moveDirection * moveSpeed *
Time.deltaTime);  // Move the player object

    }

}
```

Explanation of Code:

- **moveSpeed** is a public variable that defines how fast the player moves. We can adjust this value in Unity's Inspector.

- **Input.GetAxis("Horizontal")** and **Input.GetAxis("Vertical")** are used to get input from the keyboard. "Horizontal" corresponds to the left and right arrow keys or the A/D keys, and "Vertical" corresponds to the up and down arrow keys or the W/S keys.

- **Vector3** is a structure that represents 3D coordinates (x, y, z). We use it here to define the direction in which the player should move.

- **transform.Translate()** moves the player object by a specified amount, based on the direction and speed.

3. **Attach the Script to a GameObject:**

    o Go back to Unity and select a GameObject (such as a Cube or a Character) in the **Hierarchy**.

    o Drag the PlayerMovement script from the **Project Panel** and drop it onto the GameObject in the **Inspector**.

- You'll now see the moveSpeed variable in the Inspector, where you can adjust the speed of the player's movement.

4. **Test the Script:**

   - Click the **Play** button in Unity to run the game.

   - Use the arrow keys or the WASD keys to move the player object around the scene.

   - You should see the player object move according to the input.

Real-World Example: Coding is Like Giving Instructions to a Robot

A good way to think about C# code is like giving instructions to a robot or a machine. Each line of code tells the game (the "robot") what to do and when to do it. When you write a script in Unity, you're essentially creating a set of step-by-step instructions for the game engine to follow.

For instance, in the **PlayerMovement** script, you are giving the game instructions like:

- "Check if the player presses the arrow keys or WASD keys."

- "If they do, move the player in that direction."

- "Make sure to move the player at the specified speed."

By using C#, you're providing the game engine with these clear, logical instructions so that the game knows how to react to player input, how to animate characters, and how to control the gameplay experience. The power of C# in Unity comes from its ability to tell the game exactly how things should work—just like telling a robot to move forward, jump, or spin around.

In this chapter, we've learned the basics of C# programming for Unity. From understanding variables and functions to writing our first C# script, you've taken your first steps toward game development. As you continue learning, you'll see how these basic concepts can be combined to create more complex behaviors, interactions, and mechanics in your game.

Chapter 3: Creating Your First Game Scene

Setting Up a Simple Game Scene

Welcome to the next step in your Unity journey! In this chapter, we'll dive into creating your very first simple game scene. You'll learn how to set up basic 3D objects, place them in your scene, and manipulate them using Unity's built-in tools. Additionally, you'll add interactivity to the scene by making objects respond to user inputs, setting the stage for your first interactive game.

The goal of this chapter is to walk you through the creation of a **basic 3D environment** using simple objects like cubes, spheres, and cameras, and then make those objects respond to user inputs like keyboard presses.

Creating Your Scene: A Basic Overview

Let's start by setting up a basic 3D game scene that includes the essential components: a player object (which will be a simple cube), obstacles (using spheres or other shapes), and a camera to follow the action. Here's a general overview of the process:

1. **Setting Up the Scene**:

   o   Open Unity and create a new project. Select the **3D** template.

- You should now have a default scene with a camera and a light source.

2. **Adding Game Objects**:

    - You can add various game objects from the **GameObject** menu or by right-clicking in the **Hierarchy** panel. For this chapter, we'll use:

        - A **Cube** as the player.

        - Several **Spheres** to serve as obstacles.

        - A **Main Camera** that will follow the player's movement.

3. **Positioning the Objects**:

    - Select the **Cube** in the **Hierarchy** and move it to the desired starting position using the **Inspector**. For example, set its position to (0, 1, 0) to place it above the ground.

    - Similarly, create multiple **Spheres** that will act as obstacles, scattering them around the scene in random positions.

4. **Setting the Ground**:

    - To provide a surface for the player to move on, you can add a large plane object:

        - Right-click in the **Hierarchy** and choose **3D Object → Plane**.

- This will serve as the ground for your scene. You can scale it to make it larger by changing its transform properties in the **Inspector**.

Now you have a basic environment set up: a player (the Cube), obstacles (the Spheres), and a ground (the Plane). You can see these objects in the **Scene view** and how they're positioned relative to each other.

Adding Interactivity with C#

Now that we have a basic scene, let's make it interactive by adding movement to the player (the Cube) using the keyboard. Specifically, we'll allow the player to move the Cube using the arrow keys or the WASD keys.

1. **Creating the PlayerMovement Script**:
   - First, create a new C# script called **PlayerMovement** and attach it to the Cube.
   - The PlayerMovement script will handle the player's movement when the arrow keys or WASD keys are pressed. Here's how we'll structure it:
     - Use **Input.GetAxis()** to capture keyboard input.
     - Use **transform.Translate()** to move the Cube in response to that input.

2. **Writing the Code**: Let's write the code for player movement. Here's a simple script that moves the Cube based on keyboard input:

csharp

```csharp
using UnityEngine;

public class PlayerMovement : MonoBehaviour
{
    public float moveSpeed = 5.0f;  // Speed of player movement

    // Update is called once per frame
    void Update()
    {
        float horizontal = Input.GetAxis("Horizontal");  // Get input for left/right (A/D or Arrow Keys)
        float vertical = Input.GetAxis("Vertical");  // Get input for forward/backward (W/S or Arrow Keys)

        Vector3 moveDirection = new Vector3(horizontal, 0, vertical);  // Direction of movement
        transform.Translate(moveDirection * moveSpeed * Time.deltaTime);  // Move the player based on input
    }
}
```

Explanation of the Code:

- **moveSpeed:** This public variable allows you to control the speed of movement from the Unity Inspector. You can adjust it to make the Cube move faster or slower.

- **Input.GetAxis("Horizontal") and Input.GetAxis("Vertical"):** These functions return values based on player input. "Horizontal" corresponds to the left and right arrow keys or the A/D keys, while "Vertical" corresponds to the up and down arrow keys or the W/S keys.

- **Vector3 moveDirection:** This defines the direction in which the Cube should move. We combine the horizontal and vertical input into a single 3D vector.

- **transform.Translate():** This moves the Cube in the direction defined by moveDirection, scaled by the movement speed and adjusted for the frame rate using Time.deltaTime.

3. **Attach the Script to the Cube**:

   o After creating the script, drag and drop it onto the Cube in the **Hierarchy**.

   o Once attached, you will see the **moveSpeed** variable in the **Inspector**. Adjust it to your preference (e.g., try setting it to 5.0).

4. **Testing the Movement**:

   o Press **Play** in Unity, and you should be able to move the Cube around the scene using the arrow keys or WASD keys.

o   You can see the movement live in the **Game view** as you control the Cube in the **Scene view**.

Creating Obstacles: Adding Spheres

Next, let's add some obstacles to our scene. These obstacles will fall from above, and the player needs to move the Cube around to avoid them.

1. **Adding Obstacles**:

   o   Create several **Spheres** in your scene by right-clicking in the **Hierarchy** and choosing **3D Object → Sphere**.

   o   Position them randomly in the scene, so they're scattered above the player. To make things more interesting, you can assign different speeds or trajectories to each sphere.

   o   Set the **Y** position to a higher value (e.g., 10) so they fall from above the player.

2. **Making Obstacles Fall**: To make the obstacles fall, we'll add a simple gravity-like effect by adjusting the **y**-position of each sphere over time. Here's how to create a script that makes the spheres fall down.

   o   Create a new script called **ObstacleFall** and attach it to each Sphere.

```csharp
using UnityEngine;

public class ObstacleFall : MonoBehaviour
{
    public float fallSpeed = 5.0f;  // Speed at which the obstacle falls

    // Update is called once per frame
    void Update()
    {
        // Move the obstacle downwards over time
        transform.Translate(Vector3.down * fallSpeed * Time.deltaTime);

        // Reset position when the obstacle falls below the ground
        if (transform.position.y < -5.0f)
        {
            transform.position = new Vector3(Random.Range(-10, 10), 10, Random.Range(-10, 10));  // Randomly reset the obstacle's position
        }
```

```
        }

}
```

Explanation of the Code:

- **fallSpeed:** Controls how fast the obstacle falls. You can adjust this value to make the obstacles fall faster or slower.

- **transform.Translate(Vector3.down):** This moves the obstacle downward on the y-axis, simulating gravity.

- **Position Reset:** When the obstacle falls below a certain level (in this case, below y = -5), we reset its position to a random location above the scene.

3. **Attach the Script to the Obstacles:**

    o   After creating the **ObstacleFall** script, attach it to each sphere in your scene.

    o   You can adjust the **fallSpeed** for each sphere to vary their speed and create different effects.

4. **Testing the Falling Obstacles:**

    o   Press **Play** in Unity, and you should see the spheres falling from above, resetting their position when they go off-screen.

o Try moving the Cube with the keyboard to avoid the obstacles as they fall.

Real-World Example: Dodge the Falling Blocks Game

At this point, you've created a simple version of a **"Dodge the Falling Blocks"** game. The player controls the Cube, moving it around the scene to avoid falling obstacles. The game could evolve further by adding more complexity, such as:

- **Scoring:** You can keep track of how long the player survives or how many obstacles they avoid, awarding points as they progress.

- **Game Over:** Implement a collision detection system so that if the Cube collides with a falling obstacle, the game ends.

- **Sound Effects:** Add sounds for when the player dodges an obstacle or when the game ends.

For example, to detect when the player collides with an obstacle, you could add a collision detection script:

csharp

```csharp
void OnCollisionEnter(Collision collision)
{
    if (collision.gameObject.CompareTag("Obstacle"))
    {
```

```
    // Handle game over (e.g., stop the game or display a
message)

    Debug.Log("Game Over!");

  }

}
```

In this chapter, we've walked through the process of creating a simple game scene in Unity. You've learned how to set up basic 3D objects, manipulate them using Unity's tools, and add interactivity with C# scripting. By following the steps in this chapter, you've created a basic version of the "Dodge the Falling Blocks" game, where players use the arrow keys to move the Cube and avoid obstacles.

You now have the foundational skills needed to start building more complex games in Unity. With this knowledge, you can continue exploring and expanding your game mechanics, learning how to handle collision detection, implement scoring systems, and create even more dynamic interactions.

Chapter 4: Working with Game Objects and Components

Understanding Game Objects and Components

In Unity, **GameObjects** are the fundamental building blocks of any game. Every object in a Unity scene, whether it's a character, a prop, a camera, or even a light, is classified as a **GameObject**. But just having a GameObject alone isn't enough to give it functionality. Unity uses **Components** to define what a GameObject can do. In this chapter, we'll explore how GameObjects and Components work together to create interactive, dynamic elements in your game.

What is a GameObject?

A **GameObject** is an entity in your Unity scene. It represents an object that exists within the game world, but on its own, it does nothing. GameObjects serve as containers to which you can attach various Components that define their behavior and characteristics. For example, a GameObject could be a **player character**, a **camera**, or a **lamp** in your game.

While a GameObject doesn't possess any actual functionality by itself, it serves as the **parent object** for all the related features and behaviors in the scene. To give a GameObject purpose and interactivity, you attach Components, like scripts, physics properties, or visual effects, to it.

Components: The Power Behind GameObjects

Components are the actual **functional building blocks** that define a GameObject's behavior in Unity. Every GameObject has at least one Component by default: the **Transform** component, which determines its position, rotation, and scale in 3D space.

You can add as many Components to a GameObject as needed. Some of the most common and important Components are:

1. **Rigidbody** – Adds physics-based behavior to a GameObject, like gravity, collisions, and movement through forces.

2. **Collider** – Defines the shape of a GameObject for detecting collisions with other GameObjects.

3. **Mesh Renderer** – Renders a GameObject's 3D model and displays it in the game world.

4. **Script** – Allows you to define custom behaviors using C# code.

Let's break down how each of these components works:

Rigidbody: Adding Physics to GameObjects

When you add a **Rigidbody** to a GameObject, you enable it to interact with Unity's physics engine. A Rigidbody allows the object to be affected by gravity, respond to forces (like a push or a jump), and collide with other objects in the scene.

To add a Rigidbody to a GameObject, follow these steps:

1. Select your GameObject in the **Hierarchy**.

2. In the **Inspector**, click on **Add Component**.

3. Search for **Rigidbody** and select it.

Once added, you'll see options in the Inspector that allow you to fine-tune the Rigidbody's properties, such as mass, drag, and the use of gravity.

For example, if you were creating a simple rolling ball game, you would add a Rigidbody to the ball to make it roll naturally when forces are applied.

```csharp


public class BallMovement : MonoBehaviour
{
    public float speed = 5.0f;


    private Rigidbody rb;


    void Start()
```

```
    {
        rb = GetComponent<Rigidbody>();  // Get the
Rigidbody component attached to this object
    }


    void Update()
    {
        float horizontal = Input.GetAxis("Horizontal");

        float vertical = Input.GetAxis("Vertical");


        Vector3 movement = new Vector3(horizontal, 0,
vertical);

        rb.AddForce(movement * speed);  // Apply force to
move the ball

    }
}
```

In this example, the ball moves according to user input
using the Rigidbody's **AddForce()** method, applying
physics to make it roll around.

Collider: Detecting Collisions

Colliders define the physical boundaries of a GameObject
for detecting collisions. Unity uses colliders to check when
two GameObjects are touching or overlapping, which is
crucial for gameplay mechanics such as character

movement, object destruction, and environmental interactions.

There are different types of colliders available in Unity, such as:

- **Box Collider**: A rectangular box-shaped collider, perfect for objects like crates or walls.

- **Sphere Collider**: A spherical collider, ideal for objects like balls or rounded shapes.

- **Capsule Collider**: A capsule-shaped collider, often used for characters or other humanoid-like objects.

- **Mesh Collider**: A more complex collider that matches the exact shape of a 3D model (though it can be more computationally expensive).

To add a collider to a GameObject, follow the same steps as adding a Rigidbody:

1. Select your GameObject.

2. In the **Inspector**, click on **Add Component**.

3. Search for the type of collider you need (e.g., Box Collider or Sphere Collider) and select it.

Colliders are essential for creating interactions, such as detecting when the player picks up an item or when an enemy character collides with an obstacle. If two GameObjects with colliders come into contact, Unity will fire collision events, like OnCollisionEnter() or OnTriggerEnter(), allowing you to respond accordingly in your code.

Scripts: Adding Custom Behavior

A major strength of Unity is the ability to add custom behavior to GameObjects using C# scripts. By attaching a **script** to a GameObject, you can define its behavior, such as movement, animations, AI, and more. Scripts allow you to tell Unity how to respond to player input, physics interactions, or other events in the game world.

For example, the following C# script moves an object back and forth along the X-axis based on time:

csharp

```csharp
using UnityEngine;

public class MoveObject : MonoBehaviour
{
    public float speed = 5.0f;

    void Update()
    {
        transform.Translate(Vector3.right * speed * Time.deltaTime);  // Move the object on the X-axis
    }
}
```

In this example, every frame, the object moves to the right (increasing the X position) by the specified speed. By attaching this script to a GameObject, it will continuously move in the scene.

How to Work with Prefabs

While GameObjects and Components are powerful on their own, sometimes we need to **reuse** the same object multiple times within our game. That's where **Prefabs** come in.

A **Prefab** is a template or blueprint for a GameObject that allows you to create multiple instances of the same object, all with the same set of components and behavior. Prefabs are incredibly useful for efficiently managing assets and ensuring consistency throughout your game.

For example, imagine you're creating a car racing game, and you need to have multiple cars in the game. Instead of creating each car from scratch, you can create a **Prefab** for the car and then instantiate multiple copies of it across your scene. Each car will have the same components (such as Rigidbody, Collider, and scripts), ensuring they behave identically.

Creating a Prefab:

1. Create a GameObject (for example, a car) in your scene by adding components such as **Rigidbody**, **Collider**, and a **CarController** script.

2. Once your GameObject is ready, drag it from the **Hierarchy** panel to the **Project** panel.

3. This will create a Prefab, which you can now reuse as many times as you want by dragging it back into your scene.

Any changes made to the Prefab in the **Project** panel will automatically update all instances of that Prefab in the scene, making it easy to modify multiple GameObjects at once.

Working with Prefabs in Practice

Let's say you've created a car prefab in your racing game. Whenever you need a new car, you can simply drag the **CarPrefab** from the **Project** panel into the **Hierarchy**. The newly created car will automatically have the same Rigidbody, Collider, and car controller script that you assigned to the original car prefab.

If you later want to change the car's properties, such as making it faster, you only need to modify the Prefab, and all instances of the car in your scene will automatically inherit those changes.

Real-World Example: The Car Game Prefab

Imagine you're developing a car racing game. You need to add multiple cars to the race, and each car has the same basic functionality: a rigid body, wheels, a collider, and a driving script. Instead of creating each car from scratch, you can create a **CarPrefab** that contains all the components necessary for the car to function properly.

Each car in the game will then be an instance of that Prefab, with the same components and behavior. You can adjust properties such as speed, turning radius, and color for each car, but all the basic functionality (engine, wheels, etc.) remains consistent across all instances of the prefab.

This approach ensures consistency across your game while also streamlining the process of adding new cars to the scene. If you decide to change how the car behaves (e.g., change the handling or make the car bounce when it hits an obstacle), you only need to adjust the Prefab, and all instances of that car will be updated automatically.

In this chapter, you've learned the core concepts of **GameObjects** and **Components** in Unity. GameObjects serve as the building blocks of your game, while Components are what give them functionality. You've also explored **Prefabs**, which allow you to easily reuse and manage objects in your game scene. This is a critical part of Unity development, especially as your game grows in complexity and you need to handle many similar objects efficiently.

Understanding how to manipulate GameObjects and Components in Unity will enable you to create interactive and dynamic environments in your games. Whether you're working with physics, collision, detection, or custom scripts, the knowledge you've gained here is essential for any Unity developer.

Chapter 5:
Introduction to Physics and Collisions

Physics in Unity

Physics is a crucial part of game development as it enables realistic behavior for objects within the game world. Whether it's simulating gravity or allowing objects to bounce off each other, physics is a tool that makes your game more immersive and believable. Unity provides a powerful physics engine that handles the underlying calculations for motion, collisions, and forces.

In this chapter, we will cover the fundamental aspects of physics in Unity, including **gravity**, **friction**, and **forces**, and then we will move into handling **collisions**—which is key for creating interactive gameplay. We'll also illustrate how physics can be applied to various game elements using practical examples.

The Basics of Physics in Unity

Unity's physics engine is based on **NVIDIA's PhysX**, which simulates physical forces, collision detection, and interactions between objects. The basic components of Unity's physics system include **Rigidbody** components, **Colliders**, and **Physics Materials**.

Gravity

Gravity is one of the most fundamental forces that affect objects in Unity. It pulls objects downward, simulating how real-world objects behave when dropped. Unity handles gravity for you automatically, but you can adjust it or disable it depending on your game's requirements.

By default, Unity applies gravity to all Rigidbody objects. The default gravity force in Unity is set to a value of **-9.81 meters per second squared** (the approximate value of gravity on Earth). This means that all Rigidbody objects will fall at the same rate, unless you alter their mass or drag values.

You can change the global gravity settings in Unity by going to **Edit > Project Settings > Physics** and adjusting the **Gravity** field. If you want to simulate a different planetary environment (e.g., Mars), you can tweak this setting to a different value.

Forces and Mass

Unity applies forces to objects to simulate movements like pushing, pulling, or rotating. A **force** is any influence that causes an object to move, and a **mass** is a measure of how much matter is in an object. Unity allows you to apply forces in various ways.

You can apply a force using Unity's Rigidbody component. Here's an example:

csharp

```csharp
public class BallMovement : MonoBehaviour
{
    private Rigidbody rb;
    public float forceAmount = 5.0f;

    void Start()
    {
        rb = GetComponent<Rigidbody>();  // Get the
Rigidbody component attached to the object
    }

    void Update()
    {
        if (Input.GetKeyDown(KeyCode.Space))  // Apply a
force when the player presses the space key
        {
            rb.AddForce(Vector3.up * forceAmount,
ForceMode.Impulse);  // Apply an upward force (impulse)
        }
    }
}
```

In this script, we use the AddForce() method to apply an upward force when the player presses the space bar. The ForceMode.Impulse makes the force applied instantly, mimicking a sudden push.

Friction

Friction is a force that opposes motion between two surfaces. In Unity, friction is controlled using **Physics Materials**. When objects collide with each other, they interact based on their physics materials, which can include friction and bounciness.

Unity provides two types of friction:

1. **Static Friction** – Friction that prevents objects from sliding when they are at rest.

2. **Dynamic Friction** – Friction that resists the movement of objects when they are already sliding.

You can adjust the friction properties of a Collider using **Physics Materials**. For instance, if you want to make an object slide easily, you can reduce its friction by adjusting the friction values in the material.

Working with Collisions in Unity

Collisions are at the heart of many game interactions. When one GameObject comes into contact with another, Unity needs to detect and respond to that collision. This is where **Colliders** and **Rigidbodies** come into play. Unity has two main types of collision detection:

1. **Continuous Detection** – Used for fast-moving objects to prevent them from passing through other objects.

2. **Discrete Detection** – Default setting used for slower-moving objects.

In this section, we'll learn how to set up collision detection, triggers, and how to handle events when collisions occur.

Setting Up Collision Detection

Unity uses **Colliders** to define the shape of an object's boundaries for collision detection. Common types of colliders include:

- **Box Collider**

- **Sphere Collider**

- **Capsule Collider**

- **Mesh Collider**

When two objects with colliders come into contact, Unity will check if they overlap. If they do, a collision event is triggered.

To add a Collider to an object:

1. Select the object in the **Hierarchy**.

2. In the **Inspector**, click **Add Component**.

3. Search for the type of collider you need (e.g., Box Collider or Sphere Collider).

4. Adjust the collider size as needed.

Triggers

A **Trigger** is a special type of collider that doesn't cause physical reactions when two objects collide, but instead allows you to detect when an object enters, stays in, or exits a trigger area. Triggers are commonly used for events like pickups, detection zones, or area-of-effect spells.

To make a collider a trigger:

1. Select the object in the **Hierarchy**.

2. In the **Inspector**, check the **Is Trigger** box in the Collider component.

You can then use the following methods in your C# script to detect trigger events:

- **OnTriggerEnter()** – Called when another collider enters the trigger zone.

- **OnTriggerStay()** – Called when another collider stays inside the trigger zone.

- **OnTriggerExit()** – Called when another collider exits the trigger zone.

Here's an example of using triggers:

csharp

```csharp
public class BallPickup : MonoBehaviour
{
    void OnTriggerEnter(Collider other)
    {
```

```csharp
    if (other.CompareTag("Player")) // Check if the object
colliding with the trigger is the player

    {

        // Perform the action, such as adding points or
destroying the object

        Debug.Log("Ball collected!");

        Destroy(gameObject);  // Destroy the ball
GameObject

    }

  }

}
```

In this example, when the player enters the trigger area, the ball is destroyed and a message is logged. You can easily expand this idea to create interactive pickups, goals, or zone detection in your game.

Collision Events

Unlike triggers, **collisions** create physical responses. When two colliders come into contact, they can push each other away based on their **Rigidbody** properties, and you can detect these collisions in your scripts.

You can use the following methods to handle collision events:

- **OnCollisionEnter()** – Called when the collision starts.

- **OnCollisionStay()** – Called while the objects are colliding.

- **OnCollisionExit()** – Called when the objects stop colliding.

Here's an example of detecting a collision:

csharp

```
public class BallBounce : MonoBehaviour
{
    void OnCollisionEnter(Collision collision)
    {
        if (collision.gameObject.CompareTag("Ground")) // Check if the ball collides with the ground
        {
            Debug.Log("Ball hit the ground!");
        }
    }
}
```

In this example, when the ball collides with an object tagged as "Ground," a message is logged.

Real-World Example: Ball Falling and Bouncing

To better understand how physics and collisions work in Unity, let's build a simple example: a ball that falls, bounces on a surface, and collides with other objects.

1. **Setting Up the Ball**

   o Create a **Sphere** GameObject in the scene to represent the ball.

   o Add a **Rigidbody** to the ball so it is affected by gravity.

   o Add a **Sphere Collider** to the ball to define its physical boundary.

2. **Setting Up the Ground**

   o Create a **Cube** to serve as the ground.

   o Add a **Box Collider** to the cube to make it interactable with the ball.

3. **Making the Ball Bounce**

   o Adjust the **Bounciness** in the **Physics Material** attached to the ball's collider. A higher bounciness value will make the ball bounce higher.

4. **Adding Obstacles**

   o Add several other **Cube** objects around the ball to act as obstacles.

   o Give them colliders so they can interact with the ball as it bounces.

When you run the scene, the ball will fall, hit the ground, bounce, and interact with the obstacles. By adjusting the ball's Rigidbody properties (such as mass, drag, or angular drag) and the physics materials, you can fine-tune how the ball behaves when it collides.

In this chapter, you learned the basics of physics in Unity, including gravity, forces, and friction. We explored how to work with **colliders**, set up **triggers**, and handle **collision events**. We also walked through a practical example of how a ball falls, bounces, and collides with other objects, demonstrating the power of Unity's physics engine.

Understanding physics and collisions is essential for creating dynamic, interactive gameplay. Whether you're building a physics-based puzzle game, a racing game with realistic car handling, or a platformer with jumps and falls, mastering these concepts will help bring your game to life.

Chapter 6: Creating Player Movement

Introduction

Player movement is one of the core mechanics in most games, and it's essential that players feel in control of their character. Whether your game is a simple platformer or an immersive 3D adventure, how the character moves in response to player input plays a huge role in the overall experience.

In this chapter, we will explore the process of creating player movement in Unity. We'll walk through capturing user input (such as pressing the arrow keys or WASD keys), implementing the movement mechanics, and using Unity's built-in components to make the character's movement feel natural and responsive.

You'll also see how Unity's physics systems and character controllers can be combined to create smoother, more realistic player movement, similar to how characters move in games like **Super Mario** or **Minecraft**. Whether it's walking, running, or jumping, understanding how to manipulate player input and physics is a key skill for any game developer.

Player Input and Character Controllers

The first step in creating player movement is capturing input from the player. In Unity, this is typically done using the **Input** class, which lets you detect key presses or mouse actions. We'll cover how to capture input from the keyboard and translate that into movement within the game world.

Capturing Keyboard Input

In Unity, you can easily capture keyboard input using the Input.GetKey() or Input.GetKeyDown() methods. These functions check whether a specific key is being held down or has been pressed, respectively. For movement, we'll focus on the common WASD or arrow key inputs.

Here's an example of how you might capture input for movement:

csharp

```
public class PlayerMovement : MonoBehaviour
{
    public float speed = 5.0f;

    void Update()
    {
```

```
    float moveHorizontal = Input.GetAxis("Horizontal");
// A/D or Arrow keys (left/right)

    float moveVertical = Input.GetAxis("Vertical"); //
W/S or Arrow keys (up/down)


    Vector3 movement = new Vector3(moveHorizontal,
0.0f, moveVertical);

    transform.Translate(movement * speed *
Time.deltaTime, Space.World); // Move the player

    }

}
```

Explanation:

- Input.GetAxis("Horizontal") and
  Input.GetAxis("Vertical") return a value between **-1**
  and **1** based on whether the player presses the
  left/right or up/down keys, respectively. This works
  for both the **WASD** keys and the **Arrow keys** by
  default.

- We then use transform.Translate() to move the
  player object based on the captured input. We
  multiply by Time.deltaTime to ensure smooth and
  frame-rate independent movement.

Key Concepts:

- **Input.GetAxis**: Captures smooth, continuous input
  (e.g., the player can hold the key to move, or press
  it multiple times).

- **transform.Translate**: Moves the object in the game world based on the direction vector calculated from input.

Rotating the Player

Often, players expect their character to face the direction they're moving in. To achieve this, we can add some code to rotate the player as they move. We'll use transform.Rotate() to smoothly rotate the player towards the direction of movement.

csharp

```
void Update()
{
    float moveHorizontal = Input.GetAxis("Horizontal");

    float moveVertical = Input.GetAxis("Vertical");


    Vector3 movement = new Vector3(moveHorizontal,
0.0f, moveVertical);


    if (movement.magnitude > 0.1f)

    {

        Quaternion targetRotation =
Quaternion.LookRotation(movement);
```

```
    transform.rotation =
Quaternion.Slerp(transform.rotation, targetRotation,
Time.deltaTime * 10f);

    }


    transform.Translate(movement * speed *
Time.deltaTime, Space.World);

}
```

Explanation:

- **Quaternion.LookRotation(movement)**: This
  creates a rotation that faces the movement direction.

- **Quaternion.Slerp()**: Smoothly interpolates
  between the current rotation and the target rotation,
  giving the player a more fluid turning animation.

This allows the character to always face the direction they
are moving in, creating a more natural and responsive feel
to the controls.

Implementing Character Physics

In Unity, player movement can be implemented using
either a **CharacterController** or a **Rigidbody**. Each
method has its strengths and weaknesses, and your choice
will depend on the style and feel of the game you're
building.

Using the CharacterController

The **CharacterController** component is designed specifically for player movement in 3D games. It handles basic movement and collision detection, but it does not apply physics forces, meaning that gravity and other forces must be manually applied.

To add a CharacterController, follow these steps:

1. Select your player object in the **Hierarchy**.

2. In the **Inspector**, click **Add Component** and search for **CharacterController**.

3. Adjust the size and center of the CharacterController to match your player model.

Here's how to use the **CharacterController** to handle movement:

csharp

```csharp
public class PlayerMovement : MonoBehaviour
{
    public float speed = 5.0f;
    public float jumpHeight = 2.0f;
    private CharacterController controller;
    private Vector3 velocity;
    public float gravity = -9.8f;

    void Start()
```

```
    {
        controller = GetComponent<CharacterController>(); //
Get the CharacterController component
    }

    void Update()
    {
        float moveHorizontal = Input.GetAxis("Horizontal");
        float moveVertical = Input.GetAxis("Vertical");


        Vector3 move = transform.right * moveHorizontal +
transform.forward * moveVertical;


        controller.Move(move * speed * Time.deltaTime);


        if (controller.isGrounded && velocity.y < 0)
        {
            velocity.y = -2f;  // Ensure we don't keep falling
        }


        velocity.y += gravity * Time.deltaTime;  // Apply
gravity
        controller.Move(velocity * Time.deltaTime);
```

```
    if (Input.GetButtonDown("Jump") &&
controller.isGrounded)
    {
        velocity.y = Mathf.Sqrt(jumpHeight * -2f *
gravity);  // Jump force
    }
  }
}
```

Explanation:

- **CharacterController.Move()**: Moves the player character based on input, while handling collisions automatically.

- **Gravity**: We manually apply gravity by adjusting the velocity.y value and continuously moving the character downwards.

- **Jumping**: When the player presses the jump button (e.g., space bar), we apply a force upwards by setting velocity.y.

Using Rigidbody for Player Movement

While the CharacterController is ideal for more arcade-like games, a **Rigidbody** component can be used to create more realistic physics-based movement. This approach applies actual physics forces to the player object, making it feel as though it is interacting with the world in a more physically accurate way.

To use a Rigidbody for player movement:

1. Add a **Rigidbody** component to your player object (if it doesn't have one already).

2. Set the Rigidbody's **Use Gravity** option to true, so that it interacts with the gravity in your scene.

Here's an example of using Rigidbody-based movement:

csharp

```csharp
public class PlayerMovement : MonoBehaviour
{
    public float speed = 5.0f;
    public float jumpHeight = 2.0f;
    private Rigidbody rb;
    private bool isGrounded;

    void Start()
    {
        rb = GetComponent<Rigidbody>();
    }

    void Update()
```

```
    {
        isGrounded = Physics.Raycast(transform.position,
Vector3.down, 1.1f);  // Check if the player is grounded


        float moveHorizontal = Input.GetAxis("Horizontal");

        float moveVertical = Input.GetAxis("Vertical");


        Vector3 movement = transform.right *
moveHorizontal + transform.forward * moveVertical;

        rb.MovePosition(transform.position + movement *
speed * Time.deltaTime);  // Move the player


        if (isGrounded && Input.GetButtonDown("Jump"))
        {
            rb.AddForce(Vector3.up * jumpHeight,
ForceMode.Impulse);  // Apply a jump force
        }
    }
}
```

Explanation:

- **Rigidbody.MovePosition()**: This moves the player
  using Rigidbody physics, making it more realistic
  by allowing for interactions with other physical
  objects.

- **Jumping**: The jump is implemented by adding an upward force (AddForce) when the player presses the jump button, and only if they are grounded.

Comparing CharacterController vs. Rigidbody

- **CharacterController** is easier to use and ideal for arcade-style games where you want fast, responsive movement. It doesn't rely on physics for movement, which can make it easier to control, but also means it may feel less "realistic."

- **Rigidbody** offers more realistic physics interactions, such as sliding down slopes or responding to other forces (like explosions), making it ideal for more complex games where physics needs to be a part of the character's movement.

Real-World Example: Platformer Game (Mario)

To help solidify the concepts, let's consider how the controls in a classic platformer game, like **Super Mario**, work.

Basic Movement:

In **Super Mario**, the player can walk left and right using the arrow keys (or joystick), and the character will respond by moving smoothly across the screen. This requires capturing horizontal input, applying a force or movement vector, and ensuring the player character faces the direction of movement.

Jumping:

In addition to walking, Mario can jump to reach higher platforms or avoid obstacles. In Unity, jumping mechanics can be achieved by detecting when the player presses the jump button (e.g., space bar), and applying a force in the upward direction.

Gravity and Jumping:

Gravity constantly pulls the player down, so when the player presses the jump button, the game needs to apply an upward force (e.g., a **Rigidbody.AddForce()** or manually modifying the **CharacterController** velocity) to lift the player off the ground.

In this chapter, we've covered the fundamentals of creating player movement in Unity. We learned how to capture user input using Unity's **Input** system, move the player with both the **CharacterController** and **Rigidbody**, and implement jumping mechanics that respond to gravity.

We also explored how these principles are used in real-world platformers, like **Super Mario**, where responsive controls and smooth character movement are key to creating an enjoyable experience for the player.

Mastering player movement is essential for game development, and understanding the nuances of both physics-based and controller-based movement will allow you to create diverse and immersive gameplay. In the next chapter, we will dive into **camera systems and character animations**, further enhancing the player experience.

Chapter 7: Game UI (User Interface)

Introduction

A great game doesn't just rely on the gameplay mechanics; it also needs an intuitive and engaging User Interface (UI). The UI provides the player with essential information, such as health, score, and game status, and allows them to interact with the game world (e.g., through buttons, menus, and interactive elements). Whether it's displaying the score in a **racing game** or giving players options in a **main menu**, a well-designed UI enhances the overall player experience.

In this chapter, we will dive into the basics of creating a game UI in Unity. We'll start by designing menus, buttons, and other interface elements that allow players to interact with the game. Then, we'll move on to more advanced topics like displaying dynamic feedback (e.g., scores, health, and timers), which are integral parts of most games. We will also use real-world examples, including a **racing game**, to demonstrate the concepts in a way that's easy to understand and implement.

By the end of this chapter, you'll have a good understanding of how to build simple, yet effective, user interfaces in Unity.

Creating Menus and Buttons

Unity provides a powerful and easy-to-use **UI system** to create interactive menus and elements such as buttons, sliders, text, and images. These elements are part of the Unity **Canvas**, which is the main object that holds all UI components. Let's begin by covering how to design a basic menu with buttons and text, which is often the first part of any game that players interact with.

Setting Up the UI Canvas

Before adding any UI elements, you need to set up a **Canvas**. The Canvas serves as the container for all your UI elements. To add one, follow these steps:

1. Right-click in the **Hierarchy** panel and select **UI > Canvas**.

2. Unity will automatically create a Canvas object along with an **EventSystem**, which is responsible for handling input events like button clicks.

3. Inside the Canvas, you can create various UI elements, such as buttons, text fields, and images.

Creating a Simple Main Menu

Let's create a simple **Main Menu** with a Play button to start the game and an Exit button to close the application.

1. Right-click on the Canvas in the **Hierarchy** panel, and select **UI > Button**. This will add a button to the canvas.

2. Select the button in the **Hierarchy** and go to the **Inspector** to customize its appearance, including text, size, and position.

3. To change the text of the button, expand the **Button** object in the Hierarchy, and select the **Text** child object. In the Inspector, change the Text component to say something like "Play Game".

Now, let's add functionality to the buttons. For example, we want the **Play** button to start the game when clicked, and the **Exit** button to close the game. To do this, we need to add some **C# scripts**.

Play Button Script

Create a new script and attach it to the **Play** button. In this script, we will use the SceneManager to load a new scene, which simulates starting the game.

csharp

```csharp
using UnityEngine;

using UnityEngine.SceneManagement;  // For loading scenes


public class MainMenu : MonoBehaviour
{
    // Method to load the game scene
    public void StartGame()
    {
```

```
        SceneManager.LoadScene("GameScene");  // Make
sure you have a scene named "GameScene"

    }


    // Method to quit the game

    public void QuitGame()

    {

        Application.Quit();  // Exits the game

    }

}
```

Now, go to your **Main Menu** button, and in the Inspector, click **OnClick()** under the **Button** component. Drag the object containing the script (in this case, the object with the MainMenu script attached) into the slot. Finally, select the StartGame() function from the dropdown.

For the **Exit button**, follow similar steps and link it to the QuitGame() method.

Real-World Example: Racing Game Menu

In a **racing game**, you would often have a start button, pause button, and exit button. A sample structure might look like this:

- **Play Button**: Starts the race (loads the game scene).
- **Pause Button**: Pauses the race and opens a pause menu.
- **Exit Button**: Closes the game application.

This simple approach allows players to navigate menus and interact with the game at the start. The next step is making these buttons more visually appealing and responsive, such as adding hover effects, changing button colors when clicked, or transitioning between menus.

Game Feedback and Score System

Now that we have buttons set up, let's focus on displaying dynamic in-game feedback, such as the **score**, **health**, and a **timer**. In most games, this information needs to be displayed in real time during gameplay. Unity's UI system allows you to easily update UI elements at runtime based on game events.

Displaying the Player's Score

To display the score, we can use Unity's **Text** component. First, create a Text element by right-clicking the Canvas in the **Hierarchy**, selecting **UI > Text**, and placing it in the upper corner of the screen.

Now, let's write a script to update the score. We will assume that the score is based on a player's actions during the game (such as completing laps in a racing game). We'll use a **public int** to store the score, which will be displayed in the Text UI element.

csharp

```
using UnityEngine;
```

```csharp
using UnityEngine.UI;  // For UI elements

public class GameManager : MonoBehaviour
{
    public Text scoreText;  // Link this to the Text
component in the Inspector
    private int score = 0;

    void Start()
    {
        UpdateScore();  // Initialize the score when the game
starts
    }

    void Update()
    {
        // In a racing game, the score might be based on time,
checkpoints, etc.
        // Let's increase the score as a placeholder
        score += 1;
        UpdateScore();  // Update the score display every
frame
    }
```

```csharp
void UpdateScore()

{

    scoreText.text = "Score: " + score.ToString();  // Update the score text

}

}
```

In the Inspector, link the **scoreText** variable to the Text component you created. This script will update the score as the game progresses, displaying the current score on the screen.

Displaying a Timer

In many games, particularly racing games, a timer is a key element to indicate how much time the player has left or how long they've been playing. Unity's **Text** component can also be used to display a timer that counts down or up.

Let's modify the script to add a countdown timer:

csharp

```csharp
using UnityEngine;

using UnityEngine.UI;


public class Timer : MonoBehaviour

{
```

```
public Text timerText;  // Reference to the timer text
element

private float timeRemaining = 60.0f;  // Start timer at 60
seconds


void Update()
{
    if (timeRemaining > 0)
    {
        timeRemaining -= Time.deltaTime;  // Decrease
time by the time elapsed since the last frame

        UpdateTimer();
    }
}


void UpdateTimer()
{
    timerText.text = "Time: " +
Mathf.Round(timeRemaining).ToString();  // Display the
timer

    }
}
```

In this script:

- **Time.deltaTime** is used to decrease the timeRemaining value, ensuring the timer runs consistently regardless of frame rate.

- **Mathf.Round** ensures that the timer value is rounded to a whole number.

As with the score, drag the **Timer Text** UI element to the **timerText** slot in the Inspector to link the script to the UI element.

Health Bar

Another critical element in many games is displaying the player's **health** or **damage status**. A health bar is often a simple progress bar that decreases as the player takes damage. You can use Unity's **Slider** component to create this feature.

To create a health bar:

1. Right-click on the Canvas and choose **UI > Slider**.

2. Customize the slider's appearance by removing the handle (if you only want a visual representation) and adjusting the fill area to represent the health.

Now, create a script that updates the slider's value as the player's health changes:

csharp

```
using UnityEngine;
using UnityEngine.UI;
```

```csharp
public class HealthManager : MonoBehaviour
{
    public Slider healthBar;  // Link this to the Slider in the Inspector
    private float health = 100f;

    void Update()
    {
        // Simulate health decreasing over time or by taking damage
        health -= 0.1f;

        // Clamp health to ensure it stays between 0 and 100
        health = Mathf.Clamp(health, 0, 100);
        healthBar.value = health;  // Update the health bar's value
    }
}
```

The health value will decrease over time, and the **Slider** component will update to reflect the current health.

Real-World Example: Racing Game UI

Imagine we are designing the UI for a **racing game**. The screen might need to display:

- **A timer** counting down to indicate the race's duration.

- **A score**, such as points earned by the player for completing laps or performing stunts.

- **A health bar** if the car can take damage from obstacles or other players.

To keep the UI clear and accessible, it's important to position each element in a way that doesn't obstruct the view of the gameplay. For instance:

- The **score** could be placed in the upper left corner.

- The **timer** could be displayed in the top-center.

- The **health bar** could be placed in the bottom-left or top-right corner.

These elements help players understand how they're doing in the game and add immersion to the experience.

In this chapter, we've covered the fundamentals of designing and implementing a user interface in Unity. We started by creating basic menus and buttons, moved on to displaying dynamic feedback like scores and timers, and wrapped up with a real-world example of a **racing game UI**. By mastering UI elements in Unity, you can enhance player interaction and provide essential information that makes the gameplay experience more immersive and intuitive.

Chapter 8: Sound and Music

Introduction

Sound is a critical component in any game. It enhances the atmosphere, provides feedback to the player, and helps convey emotions that are hard to communicate visually. Whether it's the satisfying sound of a jump, the powerful roar of a gunshot, or the background music setting the mood of the level, sound can drastically improve the player's experience.

In Unity, the integration of sound and music is straightforward, thanks to its robust **Audio** system. This chapter will cover the basics of adding sound effects, playing background music, and managing audio in a Unity project. By the end of this chapter, you'll know how to implement a variety of audio elements and control them based on in-game events.

We'll use a **shooting game** as our real-world example. In this game, the player will hear a shooting sound every time they fire their weapon, and the background music will change depending on their progress. This dynamic interaction between sound effects and background music will help you understand how to build immersive audio systems for your own games.

Adding Sounds to Your Game

Setting Up Audio Sources

To play any sound in Unity, you first need to use an **AudioSource**. This is a component that plays back an **AudioClip**. You can attach an AudioSource to any GameObject in your scene, and it will be responsible for playing sound through that object.

Here's how to add an AudioSource to your project:

1. **Create a GameObject** (e.g., a player or a weapon) in the **Hierarchy** panel.

2. **Add an AudioSource component** to the object by selecting it, then clicking **Add Component** in the Inspector and searching for **AudioSource**.

3. In the **AudioSource** component, you can assign an **AudioClip** (the actual sound file) and adjust the settings such as **volume**, **pitch**, and whether the sound should **loop** or not.

Playing Sound Effects for Actions

A common scenario in many games is the use of sound effects for specific actions. For example, in a shooting game, you'd want to play a **shooting sound** every time the player fires their weapon.

To achieve this, you can write a simple script that triggers the sound when the player presses a button to shoot. Here's an example using a **gunshot sound**:

csharp

```csharp
using UnityEngine;

public class Shooting : MonoBehaviour
{
    public AudioSource shootSound;  // Drag the AudioSource here in the Inspector
    public AudioClip shootClip;    // Drag the gunshot audio clip here

    void Update()
    {
        if (Input.GetButtonDown("Fire1")) // "Fire1" is typically set to the left mouse button
        {
            Shoot();
        }
    }

    void Shoot()
    {
        shootSound.PlayOneShot(shootClip); // Play the shooting sound once
    }
```

}

In this script:

- **AudioSource.PlayOneShot()** is used to play the sound effect without interrupting any other sounds that might already be playing.

- The **shootClip** represents the sound that will be played, which you assign through the **Inspector**.

You can use similar logic for other actions, such as:

- **Jumping**: Play a jumping sound when the player presses the jump button.

- **Hitting an enemy**: Play a sound when the player's attack hits an enemy.

Adding Background Music

Background music (BGM) helps set the tone of the game. For example, in a fast-paced action scene, you might have intense music, whereas in a calm area, you might use more ambient music. Unity makes it easy to loop background music throughout the game.

To add background music:

1. Import the audio clip into your project.

2. Create an empty **GameObject** called something like "MusicManager" to hold the background music.

3. Add an **AudioSource** to this GameObject and assign the music clip.

4. Make sure that the **Loop** property of the AudioSource is enabled, so the music will continue to play until you change it.

Here's how you might implement background music in a script:

csharp

```csharp
using UnityEngine;

public class MusicManager : MonoBehaviour
{
    public AudioSource musicSource;  // The AudioSource that plays the music

    public AudioClip mainMusic;      // The main background music clip

    public AudioClip battleMusic;    // A different music clip for when battle begins

    void Start()
    {
        // Start with the main background music
        musicSource.clip = mainMusic;
        musicSource.Play();
    }
}
```

```
public void SwitchToBattleMusic()

{

    // Switch to the battle music

    musicSource.clip = battleMusic;

    musicSource.Play();

}


public void SwitchToMainMusic()

{

    // Switch back to the main background music

    musicSource.clip = mainMusic;

    musicSource.Play();

}

}
```

In this example:

- The **MusicManager** script switches between two music clips: the main background music and battle music.

- The **SwitchToBattleMusic()** function changes the music when a battle starts, and the **SwitchToMainMusic()** function switches it back to the calm background music when the battle ends.

To trigger the music changes in the game, you can call these functions when the player enters different states (e.g., when the player is near an enemy or when the game ends).

Audio Management

In games with many sounds, it's important to manage the **volume**, **looping**, and **grouping** of audio. Unity provides several ways to optimize and control how audio behaves during gameplay.

Adjusting Audio Volume

In Unity, you can adjust the volume of individual AudioSources or apply global volume controls. This is useful for things like adjusting the master volume or lowering the sound during a menu screen.

To change the volume of an AudioSource:

csharp

```
audioSource.volume = 0.5f;  // Set volume to 50%
```

For global volume control, you can manipulate Unity's **AudioListener** component. For example, you can create a script to adjust the volume during gameplay based on player input:

csharp

```
using UnityEngine;
```

```
public class VolumeControl : MonoBehaviour
{
    public AudioListener gameListener;

    void Update()
    {
        float volume = Input.GetAxis("Volume");  // Use axis input or sliders for volume control
        AudioListener.volume = Mathf.Clamp(volume, 0.0f, 1.0f);  // Adjust volume
    }
}
```

Here, we modify the volume of all audio in the game using the **AudioListener.volume** property. **Mathf.Clamp** ensures the volume stays between 0 (mute) and 1 (max volume).

Audio Mixing and Groups

When managing many sound effects, it's useful to group them based on their category or importance. For instance, in a **shooting game**, you might have different groups for **effects**, **ambient sounds**, and **music**. Unity's **Audio Mixer** lets you control groups of audio and apply effects like reverb or EQ.

To create and manage audio groups:

1. Go to **Window** > **Audio** > **Audio Mixer**.

2. In the Audio Mixer window, create a new mixer.

3. Drag different AudioSources (e.g., music, sound effects) into the mixer.

4. You can then adjust the **volume**, **pitch**, and apply various audio effects to the groups.

This lets you easily balance the sound levels and make adjustments on the fly, without affecting individual sounds directly.

Real-World Example: A Shooting Game's Sound System

Let's now focus on how sound works in a **shooting game**, where the audio feedback is crucial for immersion. In this type of game, we might need several different types of sounds:

- **Gunshot sounds**: A distinct sound when the player shoots their weapon.

- **Reload sounds**: A sound when the player reloads the weapon.

- **Ambient sounds**: Background music that changes based on the player's progress (e.g., more intense music when enemies are nearby).

- **Impact sounds**: A sound when a bullet hits an object or an enemy.

We can apply the techniques we learned in this chapter to manage all these sounds. For example:

- Use **AudioSource.PlayOneShot** to play gunshot sounds, as these are short and shouldn't interrupt other audio.

- Use a **looping AudioSource** for background music, switching between calm and intense tracks based on the gameplay.

- Use **AudioMixers** to balance the volume of gunshots and music.

A typical implementation would look like this:

1. The **gunshot sound** is triggered every time the player fires the weapon.

2. The **background music** dynamically changes depending on the situation. When the player enters combat, more intense music starts playing.

3. When the player reloads, the script triggers a reload sound.

This multi-layered audio feedback creates a rich auditory experience that responds to the player's actions.

In this chapter, we explored how to integrate sound and music into your Unity game. We covered:

- Adding sound effects for actions like shooting and jumping.

- Setting up background music that dynamically changes based on the player's progress.

- Managing audio volume, mixing, and controlling multiple audio sources in your game.

By using sound effectively, you can greatly enhance the player's immersion and engagement with your game. A well-crafted audio experience not only supports the gameplay but also adds emotional depth, reinforcing the atmosphere of the game world.

In the next chapter, we will explore **game animations**, where we'll cover how to bring your characters and objects to life, further enhancing the player's experience.

Chapter 9: Animation and Character Movement

Introduction

In video games, animation plays a critical role in bringing the world and characters to life. Whether it's a character walking, jumping, or interacting with the environment, animation helps players understand the actions taking place and makes the experience more immersive.

In Unity, animations are typically applied to game objects using the **Animator** component and an **Animator Controller**. These tools allow you to animate both characters and objects, as well as manage how different animations blend together. This chapter will guide you through the process of creating and managing animations in Unity, with a focus on animating character movement. By the end, you will have a solid understanding of how to animate characters for your own games.

We will use examples from well-known games like **Super Mario Odyssey** and **The Legend of Zelda**, where character movement animations change dynamically based on the player's actions. This will help you understand how to implement animations that respond to user input, ensuring smooth transitions between different actions.

Animating Characters

Animating characters involves creating a series of frames or poses that represent the character's movements over time. Unity provides a powerful system for animating characters, including the **Animation window, Animator Controller**, and **Animation Clips**.

Creating Simple Animations

Before we dive into more complex character movement, it's important to understand how to create basic animations in Unity.

1. **Create a New Animation Clip:**

   o Select the object or character you want to animate in the **Hierarchy**.

   o In the **Animation** window (Window > Animation), click on **Create** to make a new animation clip.

   o Unity will automatically create an **Animator** component on your object if it doesn't already have one.

   o In the **Animation** window, click on **Add Property** to add properties like **position**, **rotation**, or **scale**. For example, if you want to animate a character walking, you might animate its **position** or **local position** to simulate movement.

2. **Recording Keyframes:**

    o   Once you have added properties to animate,
        you can create **keyframes**. Keyframes are
        the points in time where you define the
        object's state (e.g., position or rotation). You
        can move the object, change its properties,
        and Unity will automatically record the
        changes as keyframes.

    o   For example, for a walking animation, you
        might create keyframes at the beginning and
        end of the walking cycle, showing the
        character's foot placed on the ground, and
        then the next frame showing the foot
        moving forward.

3. **Editing and Fine-tuning Animations:**

    o   After creating the keyframes, you can fine-
        tune the animation by adjusting the timing
        between keyframes, which controls the
        speed of the movement.

    o   Use the **curve editor** to adjust the
        smoothness of the transition between
        keyframes, allowing you to create more
        natural movements.

For a simple **walking animation**, your keyframes would
move the character's legs and arms to simulate a walking
cycle. You could also animate the character's **head** and
torso to add realism. Once this basic animation is created,
it can be used repeatedly, either as a looping animation or
triggered by specific game events.

Looping Animations

To make a walking animation loop smoothly, you need to ensure that the starting and ending frames are consistent. This means that the final frame of the animation should match the first frame in terms of the character's position or pose. Unity automatically loops animations when they are assigned to the Animator Controller, but you can control this by selecting the **Loop Time** option in the **Animation Clip** settings.

Animator Controller: Blending Animations

The **Animator Controller** is where Unity's animation system really shines. It allows you to manage multiple animations, define when they should play, and set up transitions between animations.

Setting Up the Animator Controller

1. **Creating an Animator Controller:**

   o Right-click in the **Project** window and choose **Create > Animator Controller**. Name it appropriately (e.g., "CharacterController").

   o Drag the Animator Controller onto the **Animator** component attached to your character in the **Inspector**.

2. **Adding Animations to the Animator Controller:**

- o Double-click the Animator Controller to open the **Animator** window.

- o Drag and drop your animation clips (like **Walking**, **Running**, **Jumping**) into the Animator window. These clips are now states that the character can transition between.

3. **Setting Transitions:**

- o To make one animation transition into another, click on one animation in the Animator window, then drag a transition arrow to another animation. For example, you might want to transition from a **Walking** animation to a **Running** animation when the player holds down a specific key (like Shift).

- o You can also set conditions for when these transitions occur by clicking on the transition arrow and adding parameters in the **Inspector**.

Using Parameters to Control Animation Transitions

In order to control which animation plays, you can use parameters in the **Animator Controller**. These parameters can be set to different values based on the player's input or game state, and the Animator will switch between animations based on these parameters.

1. **Creating Parameters:**

- o In the **Animator** window, click on the **Parameters** tab and add new parameters. Common types of parameters include:

    - **Float**: For continuous values like speed.

    - **Bool**: For simple true/false values (e.g., "isJumping").

    - **Trigger**: For one-time actions (e.g., a "jump" trigger).

    - **Int**: For discrete values (e.g., "level number").

2. **Using Parameters for Transitions:**

    - o In the Animator window, select a transition arrow, and in the **Inspector**, set the conditions for when the transition should happen. For example:

        - Transition from **Walking** to **Running** when the **Speed** parameter is greater than a certain value (e.g., 5).

        - Transition to **Jumping** when the **IsJumping** parameter is set to true.

Blend Trees: Smooth Animation Transitions

To create smooth, dynamic transitions between multiple animations, you can use a **Blend Tree**. A Blend Tree is used when you have more than one animation and want to blend them together based on certain parameters. For instance, in a character controller, you may want to smoothly blend between walking, running, and idle animations based on the character's movement speed.

1. **Creating a Blend Tree:**

   o In the Animator window, right-click and select **Create State > From New Blend Tree**.

   o Double-click the Blend Tree to open the **Blend Tree Editor**.

   o Add your different animations (e.g., **Idle**, **Walk**, **Run**) and assign them to a **float parameter** such as **Speed**.

   o The **Speed** parameter controls how the blend tree mixes between animations, so when the player moves slower, the character will use the **Idle** or **Walk** animations, and when moving fast, the character will use the **Run** animation.

2. **Adjusting Blend Settings:**

   o You can adjust how much influence each animation has over the blend, allowing for smooth transitions between different movement speeds.

Real-World Example: Character Movement in Super Mario Odyssey and Zelda

In games like **Super Mario Odyssey** and **The Legend of Zelda**, character movement is not just about walking or running; it involves a range of actions that all require seamless animation transitions.

1. **Super Mario Odyssey:**

   o In **Super Mario Odyssey**, Mario's movement animations change based on the player's actions. For example, if the player holds the run button, Mario's walking animation transitions to a running animation.

   o Mario also has unique animations for actions like **jumping, crouching, attacking**, and **throwing** his hat. These animations all blend smoothly, depending on how the player interacts with the game world.

   o In this case, the Animator Controller allows for multiple actions to be triggered based on the input, such as transitioning between walking and running, or between idle and jump animations.

2. **The Legend of Zelda:**

   o In **The Legend of Zelda: Breath of the Wild,** Link's animations change depending on what the player is doing. When Link is walking or running, the animation blends between different states based on how fast he's moving.

- o When the player equips different weapons or enters different stances (e.g., sword fighting, archery, or shield blocking), the Animator Controller dynamically switches between corresponding animations.

- o The use of **Blend Trees** in Zelda allows Link's movement to feel fluid and responsive, with smooth transitions based on the player's input.

These games illustrate the importance of smoothly blending animations to reflect the character's actions in response to the player's input.

In this chapter, we covered the essential elements of animating characters in Unity:

- How to create simple animations using keyframes.

- How to use the Animator Controller to manage multiple animations and transition smoothly between them.

- How to use **Blend Trees** to create dynamic, smooth transitions based on player input or game states.

By applying these principles, you can bring your characters to life and create an engaging, responsive gameplay experience. The integration of animation and movement is crucial in modern games, and Unity's powerful animation tools make this process accessible and efficient.

Chapter 10: Game Logic and AI

Introduction

In this chapter, we'll explore how to implement game logic and create basic artificial intelligence (AI) in Unity. Whether you're building a shooter, platformer, or puzzle game, the logic that governs how your game functions is crucial to providing a rewarding player experience. Additionally, AI can make your game world feel dynamic and reactive, creating engaging interactions between the player and non-player characters (NPCs).

Game logic includes everything from the basic rules of your game (such as what happens when a player wins or loses) to managing game states (such as progressing to new levels or restarting the game). AI is the part of your game that enables enemies or other characters to make decisions, react to the player, and behave intelligently within the game environment.

In this chapter, we will:

1. **Implement basic game rules** that define the structure and flow of your game.

2. **Introduce basic AI** concepts, such as patrol, chase, and detection, to create simple enemy behaviors.

3. **Use real-world examples**, like a simple shooter game, to illustrate how game logic and AI come together to enhance gameplay.

By the end of this chapter, you'll have a clear understanding of how to implement game logic and create basic AI behaviors for enemies in your games.

Implementing Game Rules

Game rules define the structure of the game, including the conditions for winning or losing, how the player progresses through levels, and what happens when the game is over. In this section, we'll walk through the key components of implementing these game rules.

Setting Up Winning Conditions

A winning condition is the set of circumstances that must be met for the player to win the game. For example, in a shooter game, a common winning condition might be eliminating all enemies, reaching a certain score, or defeating a boss. In other games, winning conditions could be more complex, such as solving a puzzle or completing a set of objectives.

Example: Defeating All Enemies in a Shooter Game

Let's say you want to create a winning condition where the player wins the game after eliminating all enemies. Here's how you can approach this:

1. **Tracking Enemies:**

   o First, you'll need a way to track all enemies in the scene. You can create a list or array of enemy game objects that are active in the scene.

   o As each enemy is defeated (e.g., when its health reaches zero), you'll remove it from the list.

2. **Checking for a Win Condition:**

   o Each frame (or at specific intervals), you can check if the list of remaining enemies is empty. If it is, the player wins.

   o Example in code:

csharp

```csharp
public List<GameObject> enemies;

void Update() {
    if (enemies.Count == 0) {
        // Player wins the game
        WinGame();
    }
}
```

```
void WinGame() {

  Debug.Log("You won the game!");

  // Trigger win condition actions (e.g., show a victory
  screen)

}
```

3. **Triggering the Game End:**

   o Once the win condition is met, you can
     trigger actions such as displaying a victory
     message, transitioning to the next level, or
     playing a sound.

Implementing Level Progression

In many games, the player moves through multiple levels
or stages. Level progression typically includes transitioning
from one scene to the next after certain conditions are met
(e.g., defeating all enemies, reaching a checkpoint, etc.).

To implement level progression, follow these steps:

1. **Track Game State:**

   o You can use a game manager script that
     keeps track of the current level and manages
     the transitions between levels.

2. **Loading a New Scene:**

   o Unity has a built-in scene management
     system that allows you to load new scenes.
     You can trigger a level transition by loading
     a new scene when the player completes a
     level.

        o   Example in code:

csharp

```
public void LoadNextLevel() {
    int currentSceneIndex =
SceneManager.GetActiveScene().buildIndex;
    SceneManager.LoadScene(currentSceneIndex + 1);
}
```

3. **Setting Up a Restart Mechanism:**

        o   Sometimes the player fails to meet the win condition (e.g., they run out of health or time). In this case, you'll want to restart the level or reset the game to a specific point.

        o   Example in code:

csharp

```
public void RestartLevel() {
    int currentSceneIndex =
SceneManager.GetActiveScene().buildIndex;
    SceneManager.LoadScene(currentSceneIndex);
}
```

Basic AI: Enemy Behavior

Now that we've covered the fundamentals of game logic, let's focus on implementing **basic AI** for enemies. Simple AI behaviors like patrolling, chasing, and detecting the player can bring your game to life, making the player feel like they are facing dynamic, intelligent opponents.

In Unity, AI is typically implemented using scripts that control the behavior of NPCs. These behaviors can be based on simple logic, such as movement patterns, distance checks, and reaction to player input.

Patrolling: Basic Enemy Movement

Patrolling is a basic AI behavior where an enemy moves between predefined points in the environment. This can be used in games like platformers or shooters, where enemies follow a set path before engaging with the player.

Steps for implementing patrolling:

1. **Create Waypoints:**
   - First, create empty GameObjects that serve as waypoints for the enemy to follow. These points will define the path the enemy takes during patrolling.

2. **Move Between Waypoints:**
   - Use a script to make the enemy move between these points using **Vector3.Lerp()** or **NavMeshAgent** (if you want more advanced pathfinding).

- Example in code (basic patrolling using Vector3.Lerp()):

csharp

```csharp
public Transform[] waypoints;
private int currentWaypointIndex = 0;
public float speed = 2f;

void Update() {
    MoveToWaypoint();
}

void MoveToWaypoint() {
    Transform targetWaypoint =
waypoints[currentWaypointIndex];
    transform.position =
Vector3.MoveTowards(transform.position,
targetWaypoint.position, speed * Time.deltaTime);
    if (Vector3.Distance(transform.position,
targetWaypoint.position) < 0.1f) {
        currentWaypointIndex = (currentWaypointIndex + 1)
% waypoints.Length;
    }
}
```

This code moves the enemy between a set of waypoints, creating a basic patrol loop.

Chasing the Player: Reactive AI

Chasing is another common AI behavior, where an enemy detects the player and moves toward them. This behavior is commonly used in many action games, such as shooters and survival games.

To implement chasing:

1. **Detect the Player:**
   - You can check the distance between the enemy and the player each frame. If the player is within a certain range, the enemy will start chasing.

2. **Move Toward the Player:**
   - Use **NavMeshAgent** for pathfinding or **Vector3.MoveTowards()** for basic movement toward the player.

Example in code:

csharp

```
public Transform player;

public float chaseRange = 10f;

public float moveSpeed = 3f;


void Update() {
```

```
float distanceToPlayer =
Vector3.Distance(transform.position, player.position);

    if (distanceToPlayer < chaseRange) {

        ChasePlayer();

    }

}


void ChasePlayer() {

    Vector3 direction = (player.position -
transform.position).normalized;

    transform.position =
Vector3.MoveTowards(transform.position, player.position,
moveSpeed * Time.deltaTime);

}
```

In this code, the enemy starts chasing the player if they are within a certain distance, and the enemy moves towards the player's position.

AI Detection: Line of Sight

To make the AI more realistic, you can implement line-of-sight detection. This means that the enemy can only chase the player if they can "see" them within a clear line of sight.

1. **Raycasting for Vision:**
   o Use Unity's **Raycast** function to detect if the player is in the enemy's line of sight.

o   Example in code:

csharp

```csharp
public float visionRange = 10f;
public LayerMask obstaclesLayer;

void Update() {
    RaycastHit hit;
    if (Physics.Raycast(transform.position, (player.position -
transform.position).normalized, out hit, visionRange,
obstaclesLayer)) {
        if (hit.transform == player) {
            // Player is in sight
            ChasePlayer();
        }
    }
}
```

In this example, the enemy uses a **Raycast** to detect if there is any obstacle between them and the player. If no obstacle is detected, they will start chasing the player.

Real-World Example: Simple Shooter Game

Let's consider a real-world example where the concepts of game logic and AI come together. In a **simple shooter game**, enemies patrol a set path and chase the player once they come within a certain range.

1. **Game Logic:**

    o The game keeps track of the player's health and score.

    o The win condition is when the player eliminates all enemies, and the loss condition is when the player's health reaches zero.

    o The player can restart the game after dying, and level progression is handled by loading new scenes.

2. **AI Behavior:**

    o Enemies patrol set waypoints until they detect the player within a specific range.

    o Once the player is within range, the enemies chase and try to engage in combat.

    o The AI also includes basic line-of-sight detection to make the enemies react only when they have a clear view of the player.

In this chapter, we've learned how to implement key game logic and AI behaviors to enhance the player experience. By setting up win conditions, managing level progression, and adding simple enemy AI, you can create more dynamic, engaging, and interactive games.

1. **Game Logic**: We covered setting up winning conditions, level progression, and restarting the game.

2. **AI Behaviors**: We implemented basic AI for enemies, including patrolling, chasing, and detecting the player using line of sight.

3. **Real-World Example**: We used a simple shooter game to illustrate how these concepts come together to create an immersive gameplay experience.

Chapter 11: Creating Multiple Levels

Introduction

In this chapter, we'll learn how to create and manage multiple levels within a Unity game. Designing multiple levels adds variety and complexity to your game, offering players new challenges, environments, and experiences as they progress. Understanding how to transition smoothly from one level to the next is also crucial for maintaining player engagement and making the game feel cohesive.

Whether you're building a platformer, racing game, or puzzle game, the ability to create distinct levels and manage the flow of gameplay is an essential skill. We'll break down the process of level design, look at how to implement level transitions, and use a real-world example of a racing game to demonstrate how to create levels with varying challenges.

Level Design Basics

Level design involves creating environments that are both engaging and challenging for the player. The goal is to make each level feel distinct while maintaining the overall flow of the game. In Unity, a level is typically a scene that contains all the objects, assets, and gameplay mechanics for a specific part of the game. Each level should provide a different experience, whether it's through new obstacles, different enemies, or novel challenges.

Designing Unique Levels

To create multiple levels, you'll want to vary aspects like layout, obstacles, enemies, and goals. This helps to keep the game fresh and exciting. Below are some key elements to consider when designing a level:

1. **Environment Layout**:
   - The layout of each level should offer a sense of progression. You could start with simple environments that introduce basic gameplay mechanics and gradually increase the complexity as the player advances.
   - Consider how the environment will challenge the player. In a racing game, for example, the track layout can become more complex as the player advances, incorporating sharp turns, jumps, or obstacles.

2. **Obstacles and Hazards**:
   - Each level should introduce new obstacles to make the game progressively harder. For example, in a platformer, the first level might feature stationary platforms, while later levels introduce moving platforms or spikes.

o   Hazards can also vary in type and behavior, like enemies that appear in specific levels, weather effects (e.g., fog or rain), or traps.

3. **Objective and Goals**:

o   Every level should have a clear objective. Whether it's reaching the end of a track, defeating a set number of enemies, or collecting items, the objective defines the level's purpose.

o   The goals should evolve over time. For example, a racing game may introduce multiple objectives for each level: first, it's just about completing the track; later, players might need to complete the track in a certain amount of time or with minimal damage.

4. **Visual and Audio Themes**:

o   The visual and audio design of each level should reflect its theme and difficulty. A forest level might have different environmental textures, lighting, and sound effects compared to a desert or snowy level.

o   These changes help to create variety and immersion, guiding the player through a world that feels dynamic and alive.

Building Levels in Unity

Unity offers a variety of tools to create levels, from terrain and 3D models to lighting and effects. Here's how to get started building your levels:

1. **Create a New Scene for Each Level**:

   o In Unity, each level is typically its own scene. You can create a new scene by going to File > New Scene and saving it under a descriptive name, such as "Level1" or "RaceTrack1."

2. **Add Terrain or 3D Models**:

   o For outdoor environments, Unity's Terrain tool lets you create vast, detailed landscapes with mountains, valleys, and paths.

   o Alternatively, you can create environments using 3D models. You can import models from the Unity Asset Store or create them in a 3D modeling program like Blender.

3. **Place Obstacles and Interactive Objects**:

   o Use the Unity Editor to drag and drop objects into the scene, such as platforms, walls, enemies, or collectible items.

   o Each object can be customized with different materials, textures, and properties (e.g., using Rigidbody for physics-based objects or Collider for detecting interactions).

4. **Designing the Player's Path**:

   o Think about how the player will navigate the level. In a racing game, this involves placing checkpoints, ramps, and tight turns.

   o For platformers, you may place different heights of platforms to challenge the player's jumping abilities, or set up obstacles that require precise timing.

5. **Adding Enemies and Obstacles**:

   o In Unity, you can create enemies by adding GameObject components, like Rigidbody for physics, Collider for interactions, and custom scripts to control their behavior.

   o Obstacles can be as simple as a box that the player must jump over or as complex as a trap that activates when the player steps on it.

Level Transitions

Once you've designed the levels, the next step is to create smooth transitions between them. Level transitions can be triggered when the player completes an objective (e.g., reaching the finish line or defeating all enemies) or when they fail to meet the conditions (e.g., running out of time or health). Let's walk through some key elements of level transitions.

1. Loading a New Level

Unity's **SceneManager** class makes it easy to load new scenes (levels) based on certain conditions. When a player completes a level, you'll want to load the next scene.

Example: Let's assume your game has three levels. Here's how you could load the next level when the player completes a level:

1. **Add a new level:**

   - First, make sure each level is saved as a separate scene (e.g., "Level1", "Level2", "Level3").

2. **Load the next scene upon completion:**

   - After the player completes a level, you'll trigger a scene transition using the SceneManager class.

   - Example in code:

csharp

```
using UnityEngine;

using UnityEngine.SceneManagement;
```

```
public class LevelManager : MonoBehaviour

{

    public void LoadNextLevel()

    {

        // Get the index of the current scene and load the next
one

        int currentSceneIndex =
SceneManager.GetActiveScene().buildIndex;

        SceneManager.LoadScene(currentSceneIndex + 1);

    }


    public void LoadGameOver()

    {

        // If the player fails, load the game over scene

        SceneManager.LoadScene("GameOver");

    }

}
```

- o In this example, after the player completes the current level, the next level in the build order is loaded. If the player fails (e.g., they run out of time or health), the game over screen is displayed.

2. Loading a Specific Level by Name

Instead of using scene build indices, you can also load specific levels by their names. For instance, if you have levels like "Track1", "Track2", and "Track3", you can load these scenes by name:

csharp

```
public void LoadSpecificLevel(string levelName)
{
    SceneManager.LoadScene(levelName);
}
```

In this case, you can call LoadSpecificLevel("Track2") to load the second level, regardless of its build index.

3. Add Level Transitions:

When transitioning between levels, it's important to provide visual feedback so that the player knows what's happening. You can add simple animations, loading screens, or fading effects to signal the transition. For example, you might fade out the current level before loading the next one:

csharp

```
public void FadeOutAndLoadNextLevel()
{
    // Fade out the screen (using Unity's UI or Camera effects)
```

```
    StartCoroutine(FadeScreenToBlack());

    // Load the next level after a short delay

    Invoke("LoadNextLevel", 2f);  // Wait for the fade effect
to complete

}


IEnumerator FadeScreenToBlack()

{

    // Implement fading logic here

    // For example, using a UI panel with an image that fades

    yield return null;

}
```

Real-World Example: Racing Game with Multiple Tracks

Let's apply these concepts to a real-world example of a **racing game**. In a racing game, you have multiple tracks, and the player progresses from one track to the next after completing a race. The tracks should vary in difficulty, layout, and obstacles, providing the player with increasing challenges.

1. Designing Multiple Tracks

- **Track 1**: A simple circuit with wide turns, no obstacles, and a short track length.

- **Track 2**: A more challenging track with narrow roads, sharp turns, and obstacles like roadblocks or ramps.

- **Track 3**: A complex track with loops, jumps, and high-speed sections that require quick reflexes.

2. Implementing Track Transitions

- At the end of each track, the player is given a time to beat or must complete a lap within a certain time limit.

- When the player finishes, they are presented with the option to continue to the next track or replay the current track if they failed to meet the time requirement.

In the Unity scene, the transitions between tracks would be managed through scripts that load the next track once the player reaches the finish line.

Creating multiple levels and managing smooth transitions between them is key to building a dynamic and engaging game. By varying the environment, obstacles, and challenges in each level, you can create a compelling experience that keeps players coming back for more.

In this chapter, we:

1. Discussed the **basics of level design**, including how to create unique obstacles, challenges, and goals for each level.

2. Explored how to **create and design levels** using Unity's scene management and tools.

3. Explained how to implement **level transitions**, loading new scenes when the player progresses or fails.

4. Used a **racing game** as an example to illustrate how levels can evolve and become more challenging.

Chapter 12: Optimizing and Debugging Your Game

Introduction

As you develop more complex games in Unity, you'll inevitably encounter performance issues or bugs that need to be fixed. Whether your game is running too slowly or you can't seem to pinpoint why an enemy AI isn't working correctly, optimization and debugging are essential skills every game developer needs to master.

This chapter will focus on two key areas:

1. **Optimization**: Techniques to improve the performance of your game, making it run smoothly on various devices.

2. **Debugging**: Tools and methods in Unity to track down and fix errors in your code or game logic.

Let's explore each of these areas in-depth, providing practical advice and tools to ensure your game runs efficiently and is free from bugs.

Optimization Techniques

Optimization is all about ensuring that your game runs as smoothly as possible without overloading the player's hardware. Unity offers several ways to optimize your game, from reducing asset size to optimizing game logic.

1. Asset Optimization

One of the first steps in optimizing your game is to focus on the assets—textures, models, audio files, and animations. High-resolution textures, complex models, and large audio files can cause performance bottlenecks, especially when targeting mobile devices or lower-end PCs.

Here are some asset optimization techniques:

- **Texture Compression**: Unity supports a variety of texture compression formats (like DXT for PC or ETC2 for mobile). By reducing the resolution or compressing textures, you can greatly reduce memory usage without compromising visual quality too much.

How to Compress Textures in Unity:

1. Select the texture in the Project panel.

2. In the Inspector, under Texture Import Settings, change the Texture Type to Sprite or Default.

3. Set the Compression to the appropriate format (e.g., DXT for desktop or ASTC for mobile).

4. Adjust the Max Size to reduce the texture resolution if needed.

- **Mesh Optimization**: Complex 3D models with excessive polygon counts can significantly reduce performance. Try to reduce the polygon count for models that are far from the camera or use lower-resolution versions for mobile devices.

How to Reduce Polygon Count:

- o Use tools like **ProBuilder** or **Mesh Compression** in Unity to reduce polygon complexity.

- o Alternatively, use **Level of Detail (LOD)** techniques to swap high-detail models for simpler versions when the object is far from the camera.

- **Audio Optimization**: Large audio files, especially uncompressed formats, can increase load times and memory usage.

- o Compress audio files to a format like MP3 or Ogg Vorbis, which reduce file sizes without losing much quality.

- o **Streaming**: For longer audio files (such as background music), stream the audio instead of loading it entirely into memory. This is especially useful for mobile games.

- **Texture Atlases**: If you have many small textures (like icons, buttons, or various environmental elements), consider combining them into a single texture atlas. This reduces the number of draw calls, improving performance.

How to Use Texture Atlases:

- o Unity's **Sprite Packer** can automatically combine textures into a single atlas, allowing the engine to render multiple objects with fewer draw calls.

2. Efficient Coding Practices

While optimizing assets is crucial, your code also plays a significant role in game performance. Poorly optimized code can cause high CPU usage, memory leaks, or frame rate drops.

Here are some coding practices that can help optimize your game:

- **Object Pooling**: Frequently instantiating and destroying objects, like bullets or enemies, can cause performance issues. Instead, use object pooling, which reuses objects rather than creating new ones.

How to Implement Object Pooling:

- o Create a pool of objects at the start of the game (e.g., bullets).

- o When an object is needed, take one from the pool rather than instantiating a new one.

- o When the object is no longer needed, return it to the pool instead of destroying it.

- **Avoiding Frequent GetComponent Calls**: Unity's GetComponent<T>() function can be slow, especially if called frequently (e.g., every frame). Cache references to components in variables instead of calling GetComponent repeatedly.

- **Reducing Physics Calculations**: Physics can be computationally expensive, so you should minimize unnecessary calculations. For example, avoid using Rigidbody physics on objects that don't need it, or disable physics for objects that aren't actively involved in the gameplay (e.g., background elements).

- **Use FixedUpdate for Physics**: For physics-related calculations, always use the FixedUpdate method instead of Update. FixedUpdate runs at a consistent rate, which is more efficient for physics simulations.

Example:

csharp

```
void FixedUpdate() {

    // Physics-related code here

}
```

- **Culling and LOD**: Unity provides **frustum culling**, which automatically hides objects outside the camera's view. You can further optimize this by using Level of Detail (LOD) techniques to swap between high-poly and low-poly models depending on the object's distance from the camera.

3. Scene Optimization

Scenes in Unity can become very large, especially if they contain many objects, lights, and animations. Optimizing your scenes helps prevent slowdowns, especially when loading or transitioning between scenes.

- **Occlusion Culling**: Unity's **Occlusion Culling** system automatically hides objects that are not visible to the camera, reducing the number of objects that need to be rendered. This is particularly useful in large, complex environments.

How to Enable Occlusion Culling:

1. Go to the Window menu in Unity and open the Occlusion Culling panel.

2. Generate the occlusion data by clicking Bake. Unity will calculate which objects can be seen and which can be hidden.

- **Baking Lighting**: Dynamic lighting can be taxing on performance. By baking static lights, you can pre-compute lighting data and apply it as textures, reducing the computational load.

How to Bake Lighting:

o Select your scene's light source and enable **Baked Lighting** under Lighting Settings.

o Bake your scene by going to Window > Rendering > Lighting Settings and pressing the Bake button.

Debugging Tools in Unity

Even the best code can contain bugs, so understanding how to debug effectively in Unity is crucial. Unity offers a variety of tools and features to help you track down errors, fix issues, and improve the stability of your game.

1. Unity Console

The Unity Console is your first line of defense when it comes to debugging. It displays warnings, errors, and logs from your game, allowing you to quickly identify issues. Here's how to use the Console:

- **Viewing Logs**: Any Debug.Log() statements you use in your scripts will appear in the console.

- **Error and Warning Messages**: Unity will show error messages when there's an issue in your code (e.g., a syntax error) or when something in the game behaves unexpectedly.

Example:

csharp

```
Debug.Log("Player position: " + transform.position);
```

- **Filtering Logs**: Use the filtering options in the Console to show only relevant messages (Errors, Warnings, or Logs).

2. The Debugger

Unity's built-in **debugger** allows you to step through your code line by line, inspect variables, and examine the state of your game during runtime. This is especially useful for tracking down complex issues or understanding why certain code paths are being executed.

- **Breakpoints**: You can set breakpoints in your code (using Visual Studio or your preferred IDE) to pause execution at specific points and inspect variables.

- **Watch Variables**: You can watch variables in real-time and check how their values change during gameplay.

3. Profiler

The **Profiler** is one of Unity's most powerful debugging tools. It gives you an in-depth view of your game's performance, breaking it down by CPU usage, memory allocation, and rendering performance.

- **Analyzing CPU Usage**: Use the Profiler to identify which parts of your game are consuming the most CPU power. You can see how long each function takes to run and pinpoint performance bottlenecks.

- **Memory Usage**: The Profiler can show how much memory your game is using. Look for memory leaks (unreleased objects) and high memory consumption that could impact performance.

- **Rendering Performance**: You can analyze how efficiently your game is rendering, including frame rate drops and the impact of various assets on rendering time.

4. Visual Debugging

Unity also offers visual debugging tools that allow you to see what's happening in your scene during runtime.

- **Gizmos**: Gizmos are visual cues in the Scene view, which can display information such as raycast paths, collider boundaries, or the player's current position.

Example:

csharp

```
void OnDrawGizmos() {

    Gizmos.color = Color.red;

    Gizmos.DrawWireSphere(transform.position, 5f); // Draws a red sphere around the player

}
```

- **Debugging Physics**: If you're having issues with physics interactions, you can visualize colliders and rigidbody forces using Gizmos or debug lines.

In this chapter, we covered key techniques for both **optimizing** and **debugging** your Unity games. Performance optimization ensures that your game runs smoothly on different platforms, while debugging tools help you identify and fix any errors in your game's code or logic. By mastering these skills, you'll be able to create polished, professional-level games that run efficiently and are free from bugs.

Chapter 13: Publishing Your Game

Introduction

Once your game is polished, optimized, and free from bugs, the next step is to release it to the world. Publishing a game involves exporting it to various platforms, making sure it meets all the requirements, and preparing it for distribution. Unity provides powerful tools to export games to a wide variety of platforms such as Windows, macOS, Android, iOS, WebGL, and more.

In this chapter, we will explore how to export your Unity game for different platforms, as well as the final steps needed to prepare your game for release. Whether you're targeting desktop, mobile, or web platforms, understanding how to correctly configure your project for each target is crucial to ensuring a smooth publishing process.

Exporting to Different Platforms

Unity makes it simple to export your game to multiple platforms, but each platform has its own requirements and nuances. In this section, we'll go through the basics of exporting for various common platforms.

Exporting to Windows (PC)

For exporting your game to a PC platform (Windows), you will need to configure your project for the Windows build target.

- **Steps for Exporting to Windows**:
  1. **Open Build Settings**: In Unity, go to **File > Build Settings**. This opens the Build Settings window.
  2. **Choose the Platform**: In the Build Settings window, select **PC, Mac & Linux Standalone** and choose **Windows** from the list of platforms.
  3. **Set the Architecture**: You can choose whether you want your game to run as a 32-bit or 64-bit application. The 64-bit architecture is recommended for modern systems.
  4. **Configure Player Settings**: Click the **Player Settings** button to configure your game's settings, including resolution, quality settings, and more.
  5. **Build and Export**: Once you're ready, click **Build** to export your game. You'll be prompted to choose a folder where Unity will create the executable file.

- **Things to Consider**:
  - **Resolution and Aspect Ratio**: Ensure your game supports different screen sizes and resolutions. You can configure this in the

Player Settings under the **Resolution and Presentation** section.

- ○ **Performance Considerations**: If your game is resource-heavy, you may want to test it on lower-end hardware to ensure it runs well on a variety of machines.

Exporting to macOS

Publishing a game for macOS is a bit different due to the platform's unique requirements and file structure.

- • **Steps for Exporting to macOS**:
    1. **Open Build Settings**: Again, go to **File > Build Settings**.
    2. **Choose macOS as the Target Platform**: Select **macOS** from the list of platforms.
    3. **Set the Architecture**: Choose between Intel and ARM architecture (most modern macs use ARM architecture, but you can target both if necessary).
    4. **Configure Player Settings**: Customize the app's name, icon, and any other specific settings for macOS under **Player Settings**.
    5. **Build**: Once everything is set, hit **Build** to export your game as a macOS app.
- • **Things to Consider**:
    - ○ **App Bundle**: Unity will create an app bundle (.app file) for macOS. Ensure that you test your game thoroughly on macOS to ensure it works on various macOS versions.

o **Signing and Notarization**: Apple requires apps to be signed and notarized before they can be distributed, especially on the App Store. You'll need an Apple Developer account for this process.

Exporting to Mobile (iOS and Android)

Publishing games on mobile platforms involves additional steps like configuring input controls for touchscreens, optimizing performance, and ensuring compatibility with mobile-specific features like sensors and GPS.

Exporting to Android

To export your game for Android, you need to set up Android-specific settings and have Android Studio installed on your machine.

- **Steps for Exporting to Android**:

    1. **Set up the Android Build Support**: If you haven't already, you'll need to install the Android Build Support from the Unity Hub. This includes Android SDK, NDK, and JDK.

    2. **Open Build Settings**: Go to **File > Build Settings**, and choose **Android** as your platform.

    3. **Configure Player Settings**: Under the **Player Settings**, set up the package name, icon, splash screen, and other Android-specific settings. You'll also want to configure the supported screen resolutions and aspect ratios.

4. **Build the APK**: After configuring the settings, click **Build**. Unity will generate an APK file that you can install on Android devices.

- **Things to Consider**:

  o **Optimizing for Mobile**: Mobile games need to be optimized for lower-end hardware. Reduce texture sizes, use simpler shaders, and minimize the number of objects in the scene.

  o **Testing on Devices**: Always test your game on multiple Android devices to ensure compatibility with different screen sizes, resolutions, and performance levels.

Exporting to iOS

Publishing games to iOS requires a few more steps, as it involves setting up an Apple Developer account and using Xcode.

- **Steps for Exporting to iOS**:

  1. **Set up the iOS Build Support**: Install the necessary iOS build support through Unity Hub.

  2. **Open Build Settings**: Go to **File > Build Settings** and select **iOS**.

  3. **Configure Player Settings**: Set up your bundle identifier, version number, and iOS-specific settings in the **Player Settings**.

4. **Build for Xcode**: After clicking **Build**, Unity will generate an Xcode project. Open this project in Xcode to configure additional iOS-specific settings (like provisioning profiles and signing).

5. **Deploy on Device**: From Xcode, you can deploy the game to an iOS device for testing. You'll need an Apple Developer account to submit your game to the App Store.

- **Things to Consider**:

  o **Apple's App Store Guidelines**: Make sure your game follows Apple's app guidelines. This includes appropriate content, metadata, and privacy policies.

  o **Test on Real Devices**: Testing your game on actual iOS devices is critical. Use Xcode's simulator, but also ensure it works on real hardware.

Exporting to Web (WebGL)

Unity can export games to the web via WebGL, allowing players to run games directly in their browsers without needing to download anything. This is great for simple, lightweight games but requires special attention to performance.

- **Steps for Exporting to Web**:

  1. **Open Build Settings**: Go to **File > Build Settings** and select **WebGL**.

2. **Configure Player Settings**: Set up the web-specific settings under **Player Settings**, such as the WebGL template and resolution.

3. **Build**: Click **Build**, and Unity will generate a folder with all the necessary files for deployment.

4. **Upload to Web Server**: You'll need to host your game on a web server, such as Itch.io, GitHub Pages, or your own website.

- **Things to Consider**:

  - **Performance**: WebGL performance is often lower than native platforms. Optimize textures, models, and scripts to improve the experience.

  - **Browser Compatibility**: Test your game across different browsers to ensure compatibility.

Final Steps Before Release

Before releasing your game to the public, there are several important steps you must take to ensure it's ready for distribution. These steps may vary depending on the platform you're releasing on, but they all play a crucial role in ensuring your game is ready for the world.

Creating an Icon and Splash Screen

The **icon** is the first impression players will have of your game. It's essential to design a high-quality, clear, and visually appealing icon that represents your game's theme.

- **Creating an Icon**: Use an image editor (such as Photoshop or GIMP) to create an icon. Typically, the icon should be square, with resolutions like 512x512 or 1024x1024 pixels. Unity will automatically resize it for different platforms.

- **Splash Screen**: Many platforms, especially mobile, require a splash screen to appear when the game starts. This is an opportunity to add your logo or branding.

Configuring Player Settings

Before exporting your game, ensure that all of your project's **Player Settings** are configured. This includes:

- **Resolution**: Make sure the game supports different screen sizes and resolutions. Configure the default resolution and ensure your game scales correctly.

- **Quality Settings**: Set up the quality settings for different platforms, such as texture quality, anti-aliasing, and shadow resolution.

- **Platform-Specific Settings**: Each platform may require special configurations, such as configuring the Android or iOS build settings.

Testing Your Game

Before publishing, you must **thoroughly test** your game on all targeted platforms. This will help you identify issues such as:

- Performance problems, like frame rate drops or slow loading times.

- Bugs or crashes that occur on specific platforms.

- Platform-specific issues, such as touchscreen controls on mobile or resolution problems on different screen sizes.

Packaging and Distribution

Once your game is fully tested, you can begin preparing it for distribution. For desktop platforms, this might involve creating an installer or a compressed ZIP file. For mobile, you'll need to submit your game to the App Store or Google Play, and for web platforms, you'll need to host your game online.

Publishing a game is the final and exciting stage of the game development process. With Unity, you can easily export your game to multiple platforms, but it's important to understand the specific requirements for each platform.

In this chapter, we explored how to export your Unity game to different platforms, including Windows, macOS, Android, iOS, and WebGL. We also covered the final steps before release, such as creating icons, setting up player settings, and testing your game. By following these steps, you'll be able to successfully publish and distribute your game to a wide audience.

Conclusion

Wrapping Up

Congratulations! You've completed your journey through the fundamentals of game development with Unity. From the very first steps of understanding the Unity interface to creating your first interactive game, you've learned essential skills that will help you build your own games. Along the way, you've gained hands-on experience with the Unity Editor, C# scripting, game physics, animations, user interfaces, and more.

As you now know, game development is a combination of creativity, problem-solving, and technical skills. Unity, with its intuitive interface and powerful tools, makes it accessible to both beginners and experienced developers alike. By understanding how to use the Unity Editor, write C# scripts, create engaging game mechanics, and implement UI, you've unlocked the foundation necessary to build games of any complexity.

Here's a recap of the key lessons you've learned in this book:

- **Unity and Game Development**: You learned what Unity is, how it functions, and why it's the go-to game engine for developers worldwide. You now understand how to navigate the Unity Editor and use the various panels, windows, and tools to set up and manage your game projects.

- **C# Scripting**: Through the basics of C# programming, you were introduced to variables, functions, classes, objects, and how they can be used to control game behavior. You wrote your first scripts, including moving a player character and responding to user inputs.

- **Game Objects and Components**: You explored the core building blocks of any Unity game— GameObjects. You learned how to add components such as Rigidbody, Collider, and Scripts to your objects, and how to organize and manage Prefabs for reusability.

- **Physics and Collisions**: Understanding physics in Unity opened the door to creating realistic movement and interactions within your game world. You learned how to work with colliders, triggers, and Unity's physics engine to detect and respond to collisions.

- **Player Movement**: By learning how to capture player input and translate it into character movement, you were able to bring your games to life. You understood the importance of Rigidbody and CharacterController components in making character movement feel natural and realistic.

- **Game UI**: With Unity's UI system, you created interactive menus, buttons, and score displays. You learned how to provide feedback to players, manage in-game statistics like health and score, and design visually appealing interfaces.

- **Sound and Music**: The integration of sound and music into your games was explored, including how to trigger sound effects for actions like jumping or shooting, as well as managing background music to enhance the atmosphere.

- **Animation**: You were introduced to character animation, learning how to create and blend animations for smooth transitions between different movements. The Animator Controller provided the flexibility to build complex animation systems for your characters.

- **Game Logic and AI**: You began to understand the rules of game progression, such as win conditions, level transitions, and AI behavior. Basic enemy AI was implemented, enabling characters to patrol, chase, and interact with the player.

- **Multiple Levels**: Level design principles were covered, showing you how to create a game with multiple levels, each presenting new challenges for the player. You learned how to handle level transitions, whether the player completes a level or fails.

- **Optimization and Debugging**: You explored techniques for optimizing your game's performance and learned how to debug common issues. The profiling and testing tools in Unity enabled you to find and resolve performance bottlenecks and bugs effectively.

- **Publishing Your Game**: Finally, we discussed the essential steps to export and publish your game across different platforms, from setting up your project for Android or iOS to configuring player settings and creating icons for your game.

Together, these chapters have given you the tools to begin building games, whether for fun or as part of your professional development. The process of creating a game involves ongoing learning and experimentation, and now that you have the fundamental knowledge of Unity and game development, you're ready to continue honing your skills.

Next Steps: Moving Forward with Game Development

Now that you've completed the foundational steps in Unity game development, what comes next? The world of game development is vast, and there's always something new to learn. In this section, we'll explore a few ways you can continue improving your skills and expanding your knowledge as you move forward in your journey.

1. Building More Complex Games

One of the best ways to improve your skills is to practice by building more complex games. Start by creating new types of games and challenge yourself to implement features you've never tried before. For example:

- **Create a 2D Platformer**: Explore Unity's 2D tools to create a side-scrolling platformer, similar to games like *Super Mario Bros*. You can create new mechanics such as jumping, double-jumping, and collecting items.

- **Build a 3D Shooter**: Start developing a first-person or third-person shooter. Implement more advanced AI for enemies, advanced physics, and complex level designs.

- **Create a Puzzle Game**: Make a game that involves problem-solving and logic, like a match-3 game or a physics-based puzzle game, incorporating complex game mechanics such as time-based puzzles or object manipulation.

As you build, make sure to break down your projects into smaller, manageable tasks. This will help you focus on one feature at a time while learning how different game mechanics work together.

2. Experimenting with Advanced Unity Features

As your skills progress, there are many advanced features of Unity that can take your games to the next level. These include:

- **Procedural Generation**: Learn how to create random game levels using algorithms. This can help you create games with infinite replayability, such as procedurally generated worlds in games like *Minecraft*.

- **Multiplayer and Networking**: Unity provides tools for multiplayer game development. You can explore the **Unity Multiplayer Service** or learn how to use **Photon** to create real-time online multiplayer experiences.

- **Virtual Reality (VR) and Augmented Reality (AR)**: Unity has robust support for VR and AR. You can start experimenting with creating immersive experiences for platforms like Oculus, HTC Vive, or AR-enabled mobile devices.

- **Shader Programming**: Learn how to write custom shaders to create special visual effects, like water reflections, dynamic lighting, or post-processing effects. Shaders are a key tool for creating stunning visuals in games.

3. Joining Game Development Communities

Game development is a collaborative process, and joining a community of like-minded developers can help you grow, learn, and get feedback on your work. You can participate in discussions, join game jams, or even collaborate on projects. Here are some places to consider:

- **Unity Forum**: The Unity Forum is a great place to ask questions, share your work, and get feedback from experienced Unity developers. There are also specific subforums for different game types, such as 2D games, mobile games, and VR.

- **Stack Overflow**: This is a great resource for troubleshooting and getting help with programming issues. The game development tag is full of Unity-related questions and answers.

- **Discord Servers**: Many game developers participate in Discord communities where you can discuss Unity, game development, and share your work. These communities often host game jams and provide a platform for networking.

- **Reddit**: Subreddits like r/Unity3D and r/GameDev are active with discussions, tutorials, and project showcases.

- **Game Jams**: Participating in game jams like Ludum Dare or Global Game Jam can give you the opportunity to work on a game in a limited time, which can be both fun and highly educational. You can collaborate with others, try new things, and push your limits.

4. Learning from Industry Experts

Keep learning by exploring tutorials, articles, and videos from experienced developers. There are a wealth of resources available for free or for a small fee that dive into the more advanced aspects of game development:

- **YouTube Channels**: There are numerous YouTube channels dedicated to Unity game development, such as Brackeys (although no longer active, the channel has a lot of great tutorials), Code Monkey, and Unity itself, which provides official tutorials.

- **Online Courses**: Platforms like Coursera, Udemy, and Pluralsight offer detailed courses on specific topics like game AI, multiplayer development, and procedural generation. Many of these courses are taught by industry experts and can help you specialize in areas of interest.

- **Books**: There are many excellent books on Unity game development. Consider reading advanced books on game design, AI programming, or specific Unity features like **Unity 2019 By Example** or **Learning C# by Developing Games with Unity**.

5. Getting Feedback and Iterating

Building your first game is just the beginning. To continue improving, always seek feedback on your projects. Share your games with friends, family, or members of game development communities and use their feedback to improve your game. Look for bugs, improve your gameplay balance, refine the user interface, and always aim for smoother user experiences.

Iterate and evolve: Don't be afraid to make changes. Game development is an iterative process. Your first game won't be perfect, and that's okay. Keep experimenting, trying new things, and improving your skills. Every mistake you make is a valuable lesson for the next project.

Final Thoughts

Game development is a journey, and this book has equipped you with the essential knowledge to start creating your own games using Unity. As you continue to develop your skills, remember that learning is an ongoing process. Each new project, whether it's simple or complex, will teach you more about design, coding, and problem-solving. Keep experimenting, stay curious, and most importantly—have fun!

The world of game development is vast, and you are now part of a thriving, creative community. Embrace the process, keep improving, and let your passion drive you forward. Who knows—your next project might just be the next great indie game!